Drama activities for language learning

by John Dougill

Essential Language Teaching Series

General Editors: Roger H Flavell
　　　　　　　　Monica Vincent

MODERN ENGLISH PUBLICATIONS

© Text John Dougill 1987

All rights reserved. No reproduction, copy or transmission
of this publication may be made without written permission.
No paragraph of this publication may be reproduced, copied
or transmitted save with written permission or in accordance
with the provisions of the Copyright Act 1956 (as amended).
Any person who does any unauthorised act in relation to
this publication may be liable to criminal prosecution and
civil claims for damages.

First published 1987
Reprinted 1989

Published by *Macmillan Publishers Ltd*
London and Basingstoke
*Associated Companies and Representatives in Accra,
Auckland, Delhi, Dublin, Gaborone, Hamburg, Harare,
Hong Kong, Kuala Lumpur, Lagos, Manzini, Melbourne,
Mexico City, Nairobi, New York, Singapore, Tokyo*

British Library Cataloguing in Publication Data

Dougill, John
  Drama activities for language learning.
  —(Essential language teaching series)
  1. English language — Study and teaching
  — Foreign speakers 2. Drama in education
  I. Title II. Series
  428.2'4'07 PE1128.A2

ISBN 0–333–39215–9

ACKNOWLEDGEMENTS

Cambridge University Press for extracts from *Eight Simulations* and *Functions in English* by K Jones

Century Hutchinson Limited for an extract from *A Separate Peace* by Tom Stoppard from Playbill Two, edited by Alan Durband

Brian Clark for an extract from *Whose Life is it Anyway?*

Heinemann Educational Books Ltd for an extract from *Off-Stage! Sketches from the English Teaching Theatre* by Doug Case and Ken Wilson (1979)

Hodder & Stoughton Educational for extracts from *Stage by Stage* by J Dougill and L Doherty

Longman for extracts from *Kernel Intermediate* by R O'Neill, R Kingsbury and T Yeadon and from *Kernel Plus* by R O'Neill

Oxford University Press for extracts from *Advanced English Practice by* B D Graver (1986)
from *Streamline English: Destinations* by Bernard Hartley and Peter Viney (1982) and
from *Streamline English: Connections* by Bernard Hartley and Peter Viney (1979)

Pergamon Journals Ltd for an extract from *Theatrical and dramatic techniques in EFL* by L Prodromou (World Language English Vol 4, No. 1 (1984))

Terry Tomscha and Practical English Teaching for an extract from *Using Total Physical Response Communicatively* by Terry Tomscha (P.E.T. September 1984)

Every effort has been made to trace all the copyright holders but if any have been inadvertently overlooked the publishers will be pleased to make the necessary arrangement at the first opportunity.

Contents

1 Drama activities ... 1
    1.1   What are drama activities? ... 1
    1.2   Drama in education ... 2
    1.3   Drama activities and language teaching ... 4

2 Introducing drama activities into the language classroom ... 9
    2.1   Warm-up exercises ... 9
    2.2   Mime ... 13
    2.3   Role-play, improvisation and simulation ... 16
    2.4   Scripts ... 21
    2.5   Taking the first steps ... 25

3 Integrating drama activities into the language syllabus ... 39
    3.1   Vocabulary ... 39
    3.2   Structures ... 47
    3.3   Dialogues ... 54
    3.4   Free stage ... 59
    3.5   Comprehension and interpretation ... 64
    3.6   A sample lesson ... 69

4 Drama-based lessons with a script ... 83
    4.1   Working with scripts ... 83
    4.2   Choosing a script ... 84
    4.3   Handling a script ... 88

	4.4	A sample lesson	97
	4.5	Creating a script	101
	4.6	Putting on performances	103

5 Drama-based lessons without a script — 111
	5.1	Working without scripts	111
	5.2	Planning the activities	113
	5.3	Sample lessons	126
	5.4	Handling the activities	130
	5.5	Simulations	138

Conclusion	145
Bibliography	147
Further reading	149

1 Drama activities

1.1 What are drama activities?

In a training centre in Kuwait a class of students is divided into groups, each of which is animatedly discussing a management crisis. In a few minutes they will act out the scene in front of the rest of the class. In a secondary school in Spain students are in pairs, one of each pair with eyes shut and the other giving verbal instructions as to what to do. In a language school in Oxford, a group of adults are lying on the floor in silence listening to the sounds around and within them. All of these classes have one thing in common. They are all making use of drama activities.

Language teachers nowadays have a variety of means for engendering student participation and activation. These include role-play, simulation, games and a wide range of drama activities sometimes called acting, drama, drama games or, as here, 'informal drama'. In addition, there is the traditional type of drama, namely the study and performance of a play, here called 'theatre'. Some commentators have seen the two fields as entirely separate, informal drama being concerned with the participants' experience, and theatre with interpretation. However, this distinction ignores the fact that both areas stem from the same base, 'the imitation of an action' as Aristotle put it, and that both share the same elements. Heathcote (1984:158) says, 'the difference between the theatre and the classroom is that in the theatre everything is contrived so that the audience gets the kicks. In the classroom the participants get the kicks. However, the tools are the same: the elements of theatre craft.'

For the purposes of this book, both informal drama and theatre are seen as one continuum covered by the term 'drama activities'. Prodromou (1984:78) shows in Figure 1 how such activities can be classified according to formality, though it is well to remember that they do overlap: improvisation may be used as a tool in the run-up to a theatrical performance, just as a performance itself may well emerge out of improvisation.

Figure 1 Classifying drama activities

Impersonal/Theatrical	Personal/Dramatic
Reading plays	Humanistic approaches
Performing plays	Games and problem-solving
Acting dialogues	Simulation
Sketches	Role-play

L. Prodromou

In Chapter 2 drama activities are broken down into warm-up activities, mime, role-play (including improvisation and simulation) and the use of scripts. Chapter 3 looks at the integration of such activities into the language syllabus while Chapters 4 and 5 concentrate on drama-based lessons with and without the use of scripts. The putting on of public performances is covered in Chapter 4. Underlying all is the proposition put forward by Heathcote (1984:97) that 'drama is about filling the spaces between people with meaningful experiences'.

1.2 Drama in education

It was in the 1950s and 60s that the distinction between drama in education and theatre activities arose. In contrast to the earlier emphasis on the quality of performance and 'the importance of the artists' craftmanship', Peter Slade and Brian Way stressed the developmental aspect of drama and how it could be used to increase awareness, self-expression and creativity. Slade (1958) saw drama and 'play' as natural to children and believed it could be used to help the child develop through stages to maturity. Way (1967) was concerned with realising the potential of the individual, 'the individuality of the individual' as he put it. This focus on doing one's own thing led in time to unstructured and seemingly aimless drama lessons. The Drama Survey of 1968 commissioned by the Department of Education found that there was too much pointless 'reeling and writhing' and that the old structure had been dismantled without a clear and firm new one to replace it. The desire for greater content, subject-matter and pursuit of knowledge was most forcibly expressed by Dorothy Heathcote and more recently Gavin Bolton. Their concern with the social element of drama and its capabilities for allowing insights into non-personal matters has led to drama being seen as an educational tool rather than a separate subject. Bolton himself puts it like this (Heathcote: 1984, Foreword): 'There has been a shift in direction from an interest in the personal development of the individual pupil ... to the recognition of drama as a precise teaching instrument, which works best when it is part of the learning process.' In the recent influential *Drama and the whole curriculum* (Nixon: 1982) proponents advocate the use of drama to illustrate and deepen understanding of other subjects such as history and the sciences.

The value of drama as an educational tool consists in fostering the social, intellectual and linguistic development of the child. Heathcote (1984:56) has isolated the following characteristics as being particularly significant:

- drama demands the co-operation of the participants
- it draws on previous experience
- it creates situations in which there is a need for precise communication
- it is experiential, thereby affecting students in other than a purely intellectual way
- it challenges students to discover new truths or insights by confronting them with previously unknown predicaments.

Thus, drama has moved into the mainstream of general education whereby every teacher, regardless of subject, can be expected to make use of dramatic activities to further the educational development of the students. At the same time there is the realisation that different age-groups have different needs and that the use of drama must be applied accordingly. The self-discovery of younger children, with elements of fantasy and imagination, gives way later to exploration of relationships to society at large and of social issues. Whereas youngsters are more at ease with short scenes with plenty of action, older students will feel happier with more conversation and a single scene. At seven years old, children need to develop self-expression; at 17 they are ready to interpret that of others. Foreign language teachers, too, need to be sensitive to their students' ages, needs and abilities when making use of the activities in this book.

1.3 Drama activities and language teaching

'Drama is a unique teaching tool, vital for language development', G. Bolton. (Heathcote: 1984, Foreword). As we have seen, in educational terms drama simulates reality, develops self-expression and enhances value judgements. In language teaching drama simulates reality, develops self-expression and allows for experiments with language. This section concentrates on those aspects of drama activities that are of particular benefit as far as language teaching is concerned.

1.3.1 Communicative competence

With the emphasis on the communicative approach to language teaching, greater weight is given nowadays to establishing situations in the classroom in which students employ language in a meaningful manner. This derives from the basic tenet that language is above all a means of communication, not an abstract body of knowledge to be learnt. Drama activities can provide a framework in which students have a real need to communicate as in Example 1.

Example 1 Students practise the use of 'some' and 'any'.

Person A	**Person B**
You are a shopkeeper with no marmalade in stock but plenty of jam.	You are a customer. You want 2 loaves of bread, margarine and marmalade.

The dialogue that takes place will certainly provide use of the desired language within a meaningful context. If, moreover, both students are unaware of each other's role (as indeed they should be, and would be in real life), then another element of genuine discourse is introduced, namely that of unpredictability. Before the ascendancy of the communicative approach, the language classroom too often consisted of set responses, guided dialogues and clearly controlled patterns of speech. This inevitably set up difficulties when students were confronted with the real world where language was for the most part unpredictable, the same statement ('I'd like some bread, please') being greeted with any number of different responses ('Certainly. Brown or white?' 'I'm afraid we've just sold the last loaf!' 'Will small do?' etc). Drama activities help to bridge the gap between the cosy and controlled world of the classroom and seemingly chaotic composition of language in the world outside.

1.3.2 Drama and the learner

In recent years language teaching has also seen a move towards a 'wholeperson' approach and a desire to put the learner (rather than the language) at the centre of the learning process. Many modern educators, such as A.S. Neal, Hold and Cook, have emphasised the primacy of emotions and there are those who claim that no real learning takes place unless the emotions are affected in some way. Stevick (1980) argues that language teaching must appeal to the creative, intuitive aspect of the personality as well as to the conscious, rational part. The games, miming and acting of drama activities provide a means of involving a student's whole personality and not merely the thought-processing part.

Another and by no means contradictory theory is that students learn best by doing things through the target language. In many places, French-speaking Canada for example, subjects such as geography are taught directly in English. In this way students' minds are taken off the target language and acquisition of the language is held to take place more easily. Some experts have advised the teaching of arts and crafts in the language lesson for similar reasons. In recent years a method based entirely on the idea of language through action has been devised, namely Total Physical Response (Asher: 1982). In this method students act upon the instructions of the teacher ('Walk to the window.' 'Open the window.') and later give the instructions themselves. While this goes beyond the scope of drama activities, it does point to the importance of physical involvement, which is often contained in drama activities. Furthermore, drama activities also provide a physical release from the constraints of having to sit in a chair for an hour. Numbness of body can easily lead to numbness of mind! Standing up and walking about can provide a jolt to daydreams or a welcome break from the strain of concentration.

Drama activities are also an important aid in helping students become more confident in their use of a foreign language by allowing them to experience the language in operation. Awareness of the ability to use a language serves to increase motivation in that the relevance and effectiveness of the material being taught is clearly revealed. Motivation also comes through the nature of the activity itself, for a successful activity will have inherent motivation. A student excitedly telling other members of his group about a good idea for a sketch is motivated by the creativity of the task.

1.3.3 Classroom management

A further advantage of drama activities is that they can help overcome some of the difficulties of teaching mixed-ability classes. On the one hand, the sort of freer activities described in Chapter 5 allow students to perform to the limits of their language ability, whereby the more able will be free to use more sophisticated language. On the other hand, they allow weaker students to compensate for lack of language ability by use of paralinguistic communication such as body language and general acting ability. It is sometimes a revelation how reticent or slower learners can revel in the opportunity to perform with more than just the spoken language. At the same time drama activities can offer a solution to the problems of large classes, for the pair and group work involved can cater for any number of students. During the presentation stage students are more likely to be attentive because of interest in the performance of their peers.

Drama activities should be both enjoyable and rewarding if handled in the right way. They are not a magic ingredient for fun, and like any other aspect of language teaching can go disastrously wrong if not prepared for adequately. The drawbacks and dangers are dealt with in the next chapter, but let us first summarise the considerable benefits that drama activities have to offer.

- They provide a framework for communicating.
- They allow for unpredictability in language use.
- They provide a bridge between classroom and the real world.
- They allow for creativity and involve the 'whole person'.
- They provide physical involvement and release.
- They develop confidence and can be motivating.
- They help cater for mixed-ability classes and large numbers.

Points for consideration:
- The difference between 'informal drama' and 'theatre'
- The potential of drama as an educational tool (rather than as a subject in itself)
- The importance of the students' age in applying drama activities
- The value of drama activities for language learning purposes

2 Introducing drama activities into the language classroom

This chapter looks at the different types of drama activities mentioned in Chapter 1 and discusses their general application to language teaching. Later chapters will deal more specifically with their integration and exploitation.

2.1 Warm-up exercises

Warm-up exercises have been developed over a number of years in response to the realisation that one cannot simply start 'doing drama' from scratch. They are, as it were, a psychological equivalent to the physical warm-ups engaged in by sportsmen. Their aim is to foster a climate of trust, awareness and group cohesion in which creative collaboration can take place. Indeed, they are sometimes called 'ensemble-building exercises'. They also help to focus participants' minds on the matter in hand. In the language classroom, they have an important part to play in achieving an atmosphere in which genuine communication can take place. Warm-up exercises can be used at the beginning of a language lesson or before embarking on work demanding group creativity and co-operation. They can also be adapted for specific language purposes (see Chapter 3). Let us look in detail at three different types of warm-up.

(a) Introductory warm-up exercises

The purpose of these is to act as ice-breakers in situations where group members may either be strangers or not know each other well. They help to break down barriers and to bond participants in that everyone shares in the same undemanding but enjoyable experience (see Activity 1).

Activity 1 Handshakes
Purpose
   Introductions; ice-breaker
Method
1 The students stand up and move around the class in any direction they choose.
2 The teacher claps hands and the students stop and introduce themselves to the nearest person.
3 The teacher tells the students to move on after allowing 2-3 minutes.
4 The activity is repeated as often as seems desirable.
5 Afterwards the teacher sees how many names the students can remember.

Duration
About 10 minutes

(b) Verbal and vocal warm-up exercises

Communication is at the core of the actor's craft. It is of course central to language learning. It is not surprising therefore to find that language warm-ups used in drama workshops to facilitate fluency and collaboration are easily transposed to the language classroom. They are particularly useful for steering students' minds away from their native language towards the target language. Activity 2 is actually adapted from a voice training exercise for actors intended to aid voice projection.

For language students it is of particular use for rhythm and pronunciation practice.

Activity 2 Sentence-building
Purpose
  Focusing on the target language; group cohesion
Method
1 The students inhale to a count of 2 and exhale to a count of 2.
2 The students inhale to a count of 4 and exhale to a count of 4.
3 The students inhale to a count of 4 and on the out-breath say 'I live in a house'.
4 The students keep inhaling to the count of 4 but on each out-breath add another segment of the following sentence, 'I live in a house/with a red door/and a red gate/near the church/at the top of the hill.'

Duration
About 5 minutes

(c) Trust and sensitivity exercises

In drama workshops and rehearsals actors have to work together in situations that can demand close and sometimes physical collaboration. For this reason they need to build up a secure and trusting relationship with one another. Trust exercises help to foster such group togetherness. In the communicative language classroom such a relationship is equally important. Speaking in a foreign language can be almost as mortifying as acting in public. Moreover, just as actors have to work together, share ideas and accept criticism, so students need to be able to collaborate, take risks and correct each other. In a climate of mistrust and suspicion students do not want to express opinions or invest any of their inner feelings. Indeed, advocates of humanistic education would state that 'building trusting relationships and sharing oneself with others' are at the basis of the educational process and that 'having healthy relationships with other classmates is more conducive to learning'. (Moskowitz: 1978,18)

Sensitivity exercises help to raise actors' awareness of themselves, each other and the world around them. They help the actor to establish the necessary mood for creativity and self-improvement. For the purposes of language teaching they can be a useful means of getting students into the right frame of mind for the task in hand. Many of them have a calming effect and are particularly useful for quietening excited groups. They also make few demands on the participants, except that they be aware.

Trust and sensitivity exercises may involve little or no language during the activity, although language will be used in setting it up. Their value lies in the atmosphere they help create. Activities 3 and 4 are two examples, one requiring the use of language and the other silent.

Activity 3 Guiding the blind
Purpose
   To develop trust and co-operation
Method
1 The students pair off and decide who is to be the blind person and who the guide.
2 The blind persons shut their eyes while their partners give instructions to guide them around the classroom.
3 The teacher suggests various tasks that might be undertaken (eg writing something on the board, turning on the light, opening the window) or places objects such as chairs and tables around the room at random.
4 After about 5 minutes the teacher tells the students to swap

roles or change partners and repeat the exercise.
Duration
Between 8 and 10 minutes

Activity 4 Mirroring
Purpose:
  To focus minds and foster collaboration.
Method:
1 The students work in pairs. Students A and B stand opposite each other with palms facing.
2 Student A makes a slow movement with his hands which Student B has to mirror.
3 The teacher should stress that this is a co-operative exercise and that there is no merit in tricking one's partner.
4 After about 5 minutes partners change roles.
Duration
Between 8 and 10 minutes

2.2 Mime

Mime is a non-verbal representation of an idea or story through gesture, bodily movement and expression. Since it does not involve language, it may seem curious that it should be advocated as an aid to language teaching. In fact, not only is mime one of the most useful activities in this respect, it is also one of the most potent. It is also relatively undemanding. Savignon (1983:207) puts it like this (with the American term 'pantomime' used to mean 'mime'): 'One of the best introductions to Theatre Arts is pantomime. Pantomime helps learners to become comfortable with the idea of performing in front of their peers without concern for language.' While mime can be highly demanding at an artistic level, at the basic level (eg miming a stomach-ache) it is simple to do and can provide much enjoyment. Mime is often involved in warm-up exercises for this reason. Look at Activity 5.

Activity 5 Guess the situation
Purpose
   Warm-up; group cohesion
Method
1 The students are arranged in groups of between 3 and 7.
2 One person from each group goes to the teacher, who whispers a situation to them.
3 The students return to their groups and mime the situation, which the others have to try and guess. (Those miming should not speak, only nod or shake their heads.)
4 As soon as someone has guessed correctly, he rushes to the teacher for another situation.
5 The game continues until one of the groups reaches the end of the list.

Possible situations
- You're having coffee when a fly lands in it.
- You're watching a tennis match.
- You're stroking a cat.
- You're reading a newspaper in the wind.
- You're a postman putting letters through a letter-box when you get bitten by a dog.
- You're having a shower when the phone rings.

Duration
About 10 minutes

The potency of mime stems from the fact that the visual element plays such a prominent part. Research suggests that memory is greatly reinforced by visual association and that recall of language items is helped when there is an associated image. (C. Rose: 1985,62) Activity 6 shows how mime can help fix language in the mind.

Activity 6 The mime box
Purpose
To revise and reinforce vocabulary items
Method
1. The teacher places a box (real or imaginary) in front of the group.
2. The teacher mimes taking something out of the box and invites students to guess what it is.
3. The teacher asks student A to come up to the box and whispers the name of an object to him. Student A mimes taking the object out of the box while the others guess.
4. The game continues with other students miming until the list of words is finished.

Suitable vocabulary
Any concrete nouns that have been taught in previous weeks
Duration
Between 5 and 10 minutes

Although no language is used during mime, it can be a spur to language use where there is the need for explanation, both in terms of the teacher's instructions and students' discussion, if the mime involves pair or group work. It is easier and more motivating for students to generate language when there is a purpose behind it, namely the accomplishment of a task. (P. Ur: 1983,3) If the mime is then performed for others, the target language can be used for interpretation and evaluation of what has been seen. Activity 7 shows how this might take place.

Activity 7 Mimed scenes
Purpose
Fluency practice

Method
1 Students work in pairs or small groups. They are given a theme or a topic to work on and asked to prepare a short mime (not more than 3 minutes' length).
2 A time-limit of 5 minutes is set for preparation and rehearsal.
3 Students perform their mimes in turn.
4 After each performance the teacher asks the spectators to interpret what they have seen.

Suitable topics
- a burglary that goes wrong
- love at first sight
- a duel
- the strange doctor
- an incident at a bus-stop
- an argument at the cinema

Duration
Up to 20 minutes, depending on the number of students

If only one group mimes a scene, as in Activity 7, then during the approximate ten-minute period there will only have been a few minutes' absence of language. For the rest of the time there will have been a lot of intense and meaningful language, a higher ratio than for many other classroom activities!

2.3 Role-play, improvisation and simulation

2.3.1 Role-play

Assuming a role is an essential element of drama. Indeed, some theorists see it as intrinsic to all human behaviour, whether in the games of children ('You be the doctor and I'll be the patient') or the many roles that adults play each day (responsible parent, dependable colleague, jovial drinking-companion, romantic partner, etc). (Heathcote: 1984) It is perhaps for this reason that it lends itself so readily to use in the classroom: 'Role-taking is so flexible in its application in education that it will work for all personalities and under all teaching circumstances.' (*Ibid*)

The main benefit of role-play from the point of view of language teaching is that it enables a flow of language to be produced that might be otherwise difficult or impossible to create. For example the different types of register and formality that occur in language use would not normally be employed in a classroom where everyone knows each other on a more or less informal basis. Role-play can also help recreate the language used in different situations, the sort of language students are likely to need outside the classroom. (Livingstone: 1983,2-5) By simulating reality, role-plays allow students to prepare and practise for possible future situations.

Looked at in dramatic terms, there is a very real difference between the static role-plays of many coursebooks, which present useful productive work, and the more active role-play used in drama workshops. The difference lies in the presence of tension. This tension is caused by conflict of some sort, an element some see as being at the root of all drama: 'Fundamentally, the nature of drama is conflict.' (Way: 1967) Certainly a key factor in creating tension must be that of unpredictability, for if participants know what the others are going to say there can be little chance of anything but the mere exchange of words. In this respect the requirements of drama and language teaching overlap, for as we have seen earlier (1.3.1) unpredictability is a key element in language use and something students should be prepared for. By way of illustration, here are two role-plays (Activities 8 and 9). The first is undramatic in nature, whereas the second contains the seeds of conflict. Of the two, the second is more likely to engage students' minds and involve them at a deeper level. In language terms the essence of genuine communication, namely the information gap, is missing in the first role-play, thereby rendering the exchange uncommunicative. In the second role-play participants cannot predict the outcome with any degree of certainty. In the next chapter consideration will be given to ways in which dramatic tension can be catered for, particularly in relation to dialogue work (3.3) and the free stage (3.4).

Activity 8 Inviting (role-play)
Purpose
  Practice in inviting and responding to invitations
Situation
  Person A is at home and bored. He rings up person B to invite her to the cinema.

Person A	*Person B*
Say hallo.	Say hallo.
Invite B to the cinema.	Ask what is on.
Say it's the latest Clint Eastwood film.	Accept the invitation. Say that's okay.
Tell B to meet you at the cinema.	

Activity 9 Inviting (role-play)
Purpose
  Practice in inviting and responding to invitations
Situation
  Person A rings up person B to invite her to the cinema.

Person A	*Person B*
Invite person B to the cinema	You have nothing to do

| tonight. (Before you do so, decide which film it is you want to see.) | tonight. However, you only want to go to the cinema if the film is one you'd like to see. |

2.3.2 Improvisation

Improvisation is one of those words that can mean very different things to different people. For some it holds a feeling of dread because of its association with unrehearsed performance before an audience, a situation guaranteed to make most people feel highly uncomfortable. In fact, improvising is something we all do in our daily lives. In their book *Improvisation*, Hodgson and Richards define the term as 'a spontaneous response to the unfolding of an unexpected situation'. (Hodgson and Richards: 1974,2) This ability to improvise is a necessary ingredient of language use, for as we know well enough few dialogues ever follow the safe, secure paths of phrasebook discourse. Compare the rather limited scope of the responses in Activity 9 with the demands made upon the participants in Activity 10.

Activity 10 Progressive improvisation
Purpose
   Fluency practice
Method
1 The teacher introduces the situation (eg parents are having breakfast and talking anxiously about their child who has stayed out all night and not returned home).
2 The teacher invites volunteers to take the parts of the parents.
3 After a while the teacher interrupts to introduce the brother/sister of the missing child who has just woken up.

The parents engage him/her in conversation.
4 The teacher indicates that another student should join the group, this time taking the part of the missing child.
5 Depending on how things develop, the teacher might introduce other characters (eg a policeman looking for a person answering to the child's description).
6 Afterwards the group discuss what happened and try again or use a different situation.

Three points need to be made here. First, the exercise is truly creative since no one, including the teacher, knows what will happen. Secondly, the potential for conflict is well to the fore, thereby giving the exercise its own dynamism. Thirdly, there is scope for the language employed in the activity to be discussed afterwards with suggestions as to how it could be improved. Redoing an improvisation may seem a contradiction in terms, since the spontaneity of the first attempt will be lost. However, there are ways around this (see 5.4.3) and the resulting 'polished improvisation' is an invaluable reinforcement of the new or modified language.

2.3.3 Simulation

The type of improvisation that has just been dealt with is very close to what some would call simulation. The differences between role-play, improvisation and simulation are far from clear and the terms have been interpreted in various ways by various authors. Simulations are generally held to be a structured set of circumstances that mirror real life and in which participants act as instructed (often in the form of a role card; see 5.5.1 for an example). Jones (1982:5) defines simulations as 'reality of function in a simulated and structured environment'. Because they require replication of the physical circumstances, as well as behaviour, they are more difficult to set up than role-plays and often require the use of published material. Jones (1985: Introduction) makes the point thus: 'Reality of function is a key concept. In *Radio Covingham*, for example, the participants do not pretend to be journalists; they are journalists because they interview and edit.' While simulations may be used for drama workshops, they are better known for their use in general education and training, particularly in such areas as management training. As a consequence, they have been adapted for ESP where the use of realia and focus on specific language situations can be exploited to good effect. A typical simulation used in Business English would be that of a board-meeting discussing a company crisis. Rules would be allotted, an agenda drawn up and the procedures and conventions of a board-meeting adhered to. However, it is not only in ESP that simulations can be effective but also for general language learning, as will be seen in 5.5.

Livingstone (1983:1) sees a distinction between the assumption of role in role-play and simulation where 'the student brings his own personality, experience and opinions to the task'. She goes on to make the point, however, that in language teaching terms the differences between them are unimportant. There may be improvisation within role-play and role-play within simulation, but for the language teacher there is only one concern: the opportunities they create for production of the spoken language.

2.4 Scripts

Scripts are most commonly used by drama groups for the purposes of staging performance. Before reaching the performance stage the script will be handled in various ways.

First, it will have to be read, either in a playreading session or individually at home. Then it will be discussed. Before rehearsals begin, the group may decide to work intensively on one or two passages to shed light on the play as a whole. They may also make use of improvisation to this end (see Hodgson and Richards: 1974, Part 3). The actors will have to memorise the script as well as interpret it under the director's guidance. Finally, the script will be transformed into a theatrical event.

The reason why scripts are of particular value to language learners is twofold. Firstly, there is their language value. They provide a rich source of comprehensible input in language that is natural and spoken. This is in contrast to the atomistic approach of much of the language skill found in many coursebooks where language is broken down into sentences or even smaller units and, moreover, what spoken language is contained therein often takes the form of realistic (and uninvolving) slices of dialogue that have little value in terms of style or humour. Widdowson (1985) complains that textbook dialogues are realistic but dull and suggests that drama texts produce the sort of dialogue that students will more readily respond to; dialogue containing 'comedy, conflict, conviction'. Tomlinson (1985) goes even further, suggesting that the 'culturally, intellectually and emotionally neutral content of many of the current EFL course books with their emphasis on accumulating bits of language and the often irrelevant trivia of survival English' actually impoverishes the student. With this in mind, it is interesting to compare an extract from a Stoppard play with the average textbook dialogue. Note that in our example (set in the reception office of a nursing home) apart from the unusual expression 'knocked up' the language is relatively easy and is far removed from the banal and trivial textbook dialogue where the characters are flat and the action uninteresting. Here the reader is intrigued and left wanting to read on.

Example 2 Extract from
A Separate Peace by Tom Stoppard

BROWN Very nice.
NURSE Good evening . . .
BROWN 'Evening. A lovely night. Morning.
NURSE Yes . . . Mr . . .?
BROWN I'm sorry to be so late.
NURSE *(shuffling papers)* Were you expected earlier?
BROWN No. I telephoned.
NURSE Yes?
BROWN Yes.
NURSE I mean . . .?
BROWN You have a room for Mr Brown.
NURSE *(realisation)* Oh! – Have you brought him?
BROWN I brought myself. Knocked up a taxi by the station.
NURSE *(puzzled)* But surely . . .?
BROWN I telephoned, from the station.
NURSE You said it was an emergency.
BROWN That's right. Do you know what time it is?
NURSE It's half past two.
BROWN That's right. An emergency.
NURSE *(aggrieved)* I woke the house doctor.
BROWN A kind thought. But it's all right. Do you want me to sign in?
NURSE What is the nature of your emergency, Mr. Brown?
BROWN I need a place to stay.
NURSE Are you ill?
BROWN No.
NURSE But this is a private hospital . . .
  (Brown smiles for the first time.)
Playbill Two, A. Durband (Ed), (Eraser and Dunlop)

The second reason why scripts are of such value is because they offer psychological security to the student. Scripts 'answer the child's desire for structure, for a secure starting point.' (Watkins: 1981,106) In other words, working with scripts is less threatening and less demanding than many other drama activities because the content is provided rather than created. For many cultures for whom other sorts of drama activities may be alien or bewildering, scripts can offer the best way into drama for this reason.

Scripts do not have to lead to performance. For language purposes each of the various treatments by the drama group as described above has its merit. Playreading in particular can be used for several ends, chief of which is that of reading comprehension. Following on from comprehension will be interpretation and discussion not only of the content of what has been read but also of the style and characterisation. There will also be possibilities for vocabulary work deriving from the contextualised items in the script. If the script is to be read aloud by a group, the activity passes from reading comprehension and more into the realm of dramatic activity, for instead of reaction we have participation and interpretation. Opportunities for characterisation, changes of mood and pronunciation work will arise.

Whether playreading leads to acting will be up to the teacher and class. Certainly there are benefits to be had from acting out the script, whether in total or concentrating on excerpts. These benefits derive from the active and physical involvement of the participants (see 1.3.2). Spoken language, whether on stage or in daily life, is accompanied by a range of paralinguistic features which cannot be replicated on chairs and behind desks. Moreover, the language loses immediacy if it is bereft of action. 'Would you like to sit over there?' suggests an accompanying hand movement. The gesture has the effect of reinforcing the meaning of the sentence, making it more meaningful to the student and indicating to the teacher that it has been understood. In this way, the printed word is brought alive.

Acting out the script may in turn lead to performing. Again, this is by no means a prerequisite. The performance may be to other members of the class or it may be to an outside audience. In both instances there are valid objectives, both educationally and linguistically. It helps develop self-confidence, self-discipline and provides satisfaction at the accomplishment of a creative enterprise. In language terms it necessitates the memorisation and use of the target language in context. Above all, it provides a goal towards which the group can work, a collaborative and creative enterprise that involves language as the means as well as the end.

This section has dealt with the aims of applying drama activities to language learning. In later chapters the method and manner of their application will be look d at in more detail, as well as potential pitfalls.

2.5 Taking the first steps

Drama and language teaching have long been associated, yet curiously the connection has been one-sided. In most classrooms the teacher is the actor and the students the spectators. The teacher mimes when trying to explain or elicit vocabulary, acts out characters when presenting a dialogue, adds exaggerated gesture when telling a story. All of this serves a purpose of course in illustrating the subject-matter, keeping students' attention and providing a visual reference for the language-content. However, the one-sidedness of the act has its roots in the teacher-dominated classroom with the teacher-performer firmly at the centre of things. The communicative approach has led to a decentralised classroom with the accent more on pair and group work and students themselves taking a more active part in the proceedings. Drama activities have a very real role to play in such a process

Figure 2 Scripts – educational and linguistic value

	non-threatening				threatening
work with scripts	reading through the play	discussion	intensive work on scenes	rehearsals	performance
language and educational value	language input of an involving kind	language production	pronunciation	repetition of language model	memorisation of language
	comprehension work	interpretation	physical involvement	collaboration	development of self-confidence and self-discipline
	vocabulary development				

but not as much attention has been paid to them as they deserve.

The reluctance of teachers to make use of drama activities may stem from one or more of the following: fear of losing control; lack of confidence; lack of space; or student resistance. It should be borne in mind that these factors can be considerably heightened by the cultural and educational background involved. Let us take a closer look at each in turn.

2.5.1 Fear of losing control

The traditional classroom has clear codes of conduct. No one is allowed to speak or move unless so directed by the teacher. By keeping to a teacher-student channel of communication the teacher can maintain a tight grip on the reins of control. In a more student-centred classroom, however, the teacher has to rely on more subtle means, such as persuasion and personal example. In activities where students are encouraged to get out of their chairs or take part in a role-play, there can be concern about students misusing such opportunities for simply letting off steam. Playing a part can become an excuse for playing the fool. This is a quite legitimate anxiety, but there are preventative strategies.

(a) Plan carefully

'The more a lesson departs from the traditional, the greater is the risk of disorder through lack of definition.' (Watkins: 1981,1) Drama activities need just as much planning and forethought as any other activity, if not more so, for an ill-prepared lesson or vague idea is more likely to lead to chaos in the case of drama activities.

Example 3 Scenario resulting from unplanned drama activities

Situation The teacher has presented various ways of socialising and decides that a role-play would be a suitable means of giving practice in using the language input. However, the teacher has not thought the activity through.

Instructions 'Stand up, walk around and socialise with another person.'

Result The students gather in groups, look bemused and talk casually among themselves in their mother tongue.

Activity 11 shows how the teacher could have prepared the task more effectively.

Activity 11 Role-play in pairs
Purpose
   To practise the language of socialising
Method
1 Ask the students to stand up.
2 Send half to one end of the room and the other half to the other end.
3 Tell the students that they are walking down a street one day when they bump into an old friend.
4 Give the students a brief example of the sort of conversation that might ensue.
5 Ask the students to pair off with someone from the other half.
6 After 3 or 4 minutes tell the students to return to their chairs.
7 Compare what happened in various pairs.
Duration
Between 10 and 12 minutes

The clarity and precision of the preparation in the above example will eliminate much of the chaos and confusion that ill-defined ideas can produce.

(b) Make sure the instructions are understood

It is just as important that the students should understand what they are supposed to be doing as for the teacher to prepare it, otherwise the preparation has been in vain. Where appropriate it might be advisable to give the instructions in the mother tongue. Alternatively, the teacher can check comprehension by asking check questions ('What do you want to find out?' 'What sort of person are you?' etc) or by asking students to retell what they are going to do.

(c) Do not be over-ambitious

Some drama activities entail a far greater risk of loss of control than others. For example, getting students to improvise a market scene carries greater opportunities for breakdown in discipline than an exercise in which students remain seated and pass a mimed object around the class. Inexperienced or unsure teachers should avoid jumping off at the deep end with the 'high-risk' activities and stick to safer and shallower waters where loss of control is unlikely. With time more adventurous steps can be taken, but both teacher and students need to gain confidence first. 'Begin from where you are' was Brian Way's advice to prospective drama teachers (1967,28), underlining the importance of not being over-ambitious. We can take stock of the activities mentioned so far in this unit and classify them according to their 'risk' element (see Figure 3).

It should be noted that the language level required for a particular activity does not determine the degree of risk required. Indeed, some of the most 'risky' activities require no language at all. The language demand of an activity is a separate but equally important factor, for, just like any other activity, if students do not possess sufficient language competence, there is little likelihood of success.

Figure 3 Classifying the risks of loss of teacher control of drama activities

Low-risk	Sentence-building Inviting (role-play) Playreading	Students remain seated; activities are limited in terms of students' freedom.
	The mime box Handshakes	The activity is tightly structured and controlled, but students have more physical and creative freedom.
	Guiding the blind Mirroring Guess the situation (mime)	The activity is of a more creative nature and requires greater willingness to co-operate from the students.
High-risk	Mimed scenes Progressive improvisation	Students are given much greater freedom of action: the activities make considerable linguistic and creative demands.

2.5.2 Lack of confidence

Many teachers believe themselves to be unequipped to do drama either in terms of their own training or personality.

Indeed, the very word 'drama' seems to fill some with dread, much as if they were being asked to sing in public. However, the role of the teacher is very often that of an organiser and, as will be seen in later sections in this unit, some activities make no more demands on the teacher than other commonplace classroom exercises – most of the exercises are no more demanding than popular party games or role-plays. Lack of training, on the other hand, might mean that the teacher is willing to make use of drama activities but does not know where to begin. Way's dictum about beginning 'from where you are' is just as applicable here. Start with story-telling and creative work; try short mime exercises; get students to do simple role-plays; develop these into slightly longer improvisations; introduce a script; try acting it out; get students to work on creating their own sketches; work towards performing a play. All of these are gone into in more depth later in the book, but for now the important thing to bear in mind is that there is no substitute for experience and that experience should be gained step by step.

2.5.3 Lack of space

A classroom full of desks or benches is hardly conducive to drama activities. Teachers planning to make regular use of such activities should seriously consider the arrangement of furniture in their classrooms. Desks can be both a physical and psychological barrier to group work and the first matter to be resolved must be whether there is a viable alternative. In some schools it is possible to book the hall or dining-room. Failing that, perhaps the most satisfactory arrangement is to have the class sitting in a horseshoe shape with the teacher at the mouth. The desks can be pushed against the walls with the horseshoe inside them.

Figure 4 'Horseshoe' arrangement of the class

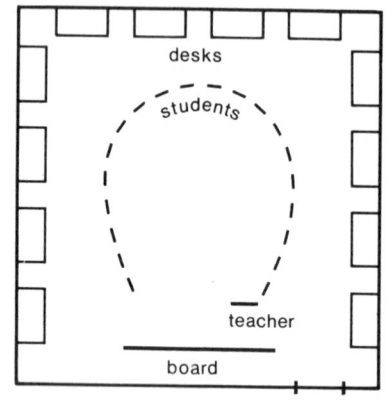

Clipboards are a useful lightweight alternative to desks for writing purposes. The advantages of this arrangement are that the students are more likely to stand up and move around than if they are slumped behind a desk. Secondly, they have a clear view of the board as well as the faces of the rest of the class. Thirdly, there is room available for one or more students to perform to the rest of the class. Appropriately, this is next to the teacher, who needs the space to demonstrate the activities. In this way the students are free of the distractions that desks can provide (books, pens, graffiti, etc) and more prepared to participate. Obviously this arrangement only applies to small classes.

There are of course many places where such an arrangement is not possible and furniture is either fixed or beyond the control of the teacher. At the very least it is important to try and ensure that there is an area of open space somewhere in the classroom where students can move about. Otherwise there is no need for extra physical features or rearrangements. Only if a performance is contemplated do props and lighting become desirable, but even then they are by no means necessary.

2.5.4 Student resistance

Student resistance to drama activities sometimes stems from the belief that such activities are trivial or irrelevant to language learning. It is important, therefore, that the teacher has a clear purpose in mind and is not merely introducing an activity for its own sake. The teacher must not only believe in the value of such activities but be able to transmit that belief to the students. One helpful tactic in this respect is to explain to the students before each activity what the purpose is. Similarly, concluding remarks afterwards can help reinforce the notion that the activity was worthwhile.

A more likely cause of student resistance is that of self-consciousness and a fear of making a fool of oneself – even when it comes to the relatively undemanding task of speaking in front of the class. Moreover, some students, especially adolescents, are naturally shy or lacking in self-confidence. Such reluctance can very quickly turn into an insurmountable barrier if students are forced to confront situations in which they feel uncomfortable. Teachers need to be sensitive to this and to follow certain basic guidelines:

(a) Lead by example

Whenever possible, teachers should themselves perform the activity in advance of the students. This not only clarifies the nature of the task but goes a long way towards reassuring the students that what is being requested of them is not unreasonable or impossible and that the teacher with concomitant authority and status is willing and able to engage in the activity.

(b) Avoid putting students on the spot

Asking a student to pretend to be a middle-aged drunk in

front of the class can have a mortifying effect, particularly if the rest of the class laugh. It might however be acceptable in a group of students that know each other well and have developed a collaborative attitude. Where students are uneasy of each other or unsure of their own ability, the teacher should refrain from making them perform in front of the class. Instead the teacher can ask for volunteers and encourage an atmosphere in which students are stimulated to put themselves forward. Alternatively, the teacher should seek to arrange things so that students perform in the relatively secure confines of a pair or small group.

Example 4

1 Good morning. Can I help you?
2 Yes. I'd like to find my perfect partner.
1 I see. Well, if you could just answer a few questions?
2 Certainly.
1 First of all, what age would you like your partner to be?
2 About 20. Not more than 25, anyway.
1 Okay. And what sort of build?
2 What do you mean?
1 Well, would you like someone who was very slim or would you prefer someone rather more plump?
2 Ah, I see. I don't think I mind, actually.
1 And what about height?
2 Oh, not too tall.

from *Stage by Stage*, J. Dougill and L. Doherty (Hodder and Stoughton)

Having decided to use the material in Example 4, the teacher should not then pick on two unsuspecting students and say, 'Come up here. Show the rest of the class how you would act out the scene.' A better approach would be to get students to act out the exchange in pairs and to enquire afterwards whether anyone would like to show their attempt to the rest of the class. Unwilling students should never be forced to perform in front of the others. With time students will gain confidence and begin to lose their inhibitions, but the groundwork needs to be carefully laid.

(c) Make positive comments

Because of their participatory nature, drama activities expose students to comment and criticism. This can make them vulnerable and it is important that the teacher is aware of this. Negative comments can have disastrous effects and will certainly deter students from wanting to repeat the activity. Wherever possible, teachers should be looking for points to praise, thereby boosting confidence. Where the teacher wishes to point out mistakes or undesirable features, it is possible to avoid direct criticism by use of implication or indirect questioning. Thus, if student A was unclear or incomprehensible, the teacher might focus on another student and ask if the class could understand him/her clearly and on getting an affirmative answer, stress to the class the importance of speaking clearly or go into the language being used. The teacher could then ask the students to repeat the activity, bearing in mind what had been said. Another tactic is to direct attention to the character in question and away from the student as such. Supposing student B has just given a poor impersonation of a doctor, standing with hands in pockets and looking lifeless, the teacher could ask the class about doctors, how they behave when seeing patients and the kind of language they might use. By a series of directed questions the teacher could lead student B to be more aware of what is required without the discomfort of direct criticism.

(d) Do not demand too much of students

Just as teachers should not attempt activities that are too far beyond their experience, so students should not be expected to engage in activities for which they have not been adequately prepared and which are thus likely to lead to their discouragement. The sort of demands that drama activities might require of students are: the risk of ridicule by the rest of the class; acting ability; use of creativity and imagination; ability to use the foreign language; willingness and ability to work as part of a group. It is just as appropriate to talk of high- and low-risk activities in this respect and for the teacher to be mindful of the non-linguistic as well as the linguistic demands being made upon the students.

In Figure 5 the activities mentioned so far are again

Figure 5 Classifying the risks for students in drama activities

Low-risk	Handshakes Guiding the blind	Low language and dramatic demand
	The mime box Guess the situation (mime) Mirroring	Low language demand but some dramatic demand
	Inviting (role-play) Sentence-building	Fairly high language demand but low dramatic demand
High-risk	Playreading Mimed scenes (preparation and performance) Progressive improvisation	High language and dramatic demand

classified according to the 'risks' they involve, but this time from the students' point of view.

Points for consideration:
- the purpose and types of warm-up exercises
- the effectiveness of mime in terms of language teaching
- the value of role-play, with particular reference to whether it is universally acceptable
- the importance of the information gap in role-play
- the nature and value of improvisation
- the value of scripts
- the treatment of scripts
- how to introduce drama activities to class work
- the reasons for and ways of overcoming teacher resistance
- the reasons for and ways of overcoming student resistance.

---

3 Integrating drama activities into the language syllabus

In the preceding chapter attention was focused on the nature of drama activities and their introduction to the language classroom. This chapter explores ways in which drama activities can be exploited in terms of the language syllabus. As has already been noted in Chapter 2, the use of drama activities should be allied to sound teaching principles and the aim of the activity should be clear to both teacher and student. The use of drama activities for their own sake or to fill up a Friday afternoon only serves to undermine their effectiveness. As a consequence, the integration of drama activities into the language syllabus is of vital importance.

3.1 Vocabulary

There has recently been renewed interest in the teaching of vocabulary. Indeed, some theorists such as Krashen (1983:155) see it as absolutely central to the language curriculum. Current thinking stresses two important factors. First of all, the learning of vocabulary is considerably enhanced by the use of aids to memorisation, such as images, mnemonics, associations, etc. Secondly, unless there is an affective element to the process there is a tendency for the vocabulary not to 'stick' (Morgan and Rinvolucri: 1986). Drama activities can help provide visual and physical reinforcement that increases involvement and helps fix the vocabulary items in the mind.

Reference was made in 2.2 to the potency of mime. Activities 12 and 13 show how easily mime lends itself to effective exploitation for the purpose of reinforcing vocabulary.

Activity 12 Vocabulary mime
Purpose
To reinforce vocabulary (after initial presentation)
Method
1 The teacher gives each student a slip of paper on which one of the vocabulary items is written or whispers to the student whose turn it is.
2 Each student in turn does a short mime to show what vocabulary item he has been given. The others write down what they think it is.
3 After the group has completed the mimes, they compare notes on what they thought the mimes showed.
Duration
From 5 to 10 minutes

Activity 13 Circulating mime
Purpose
To reinforce vocabulary
Method
1 The teacher writes down all the vocabulary items on sticky labels prior to the lesson.
2 At the appropriate point in the lesson, the teacher applies a label to the back of each student.
3 The students are asked to move at will around the room. When the teacher claps hands, the students pair off with the nearest person.
4 The students look at each other's backs. They then perform

a short mime to indicate what they have seen. No talking is allowed.
5 After a suitable length of time, the teacher asks the students to move around the room again and the process is repeated two or three times.
6 The teacher asks the students to guess what is on their backs. This is checked with their actual label.

Duration
About 7 minutes

It is not only elementary vocabulary items that can be brought to life by mime. The extract in Example 5 can be enlivened by getting students to walk around the room and to alter their walk at intervals as instructed by the teacher: 'Limp. Now march.' etc. Alternatively, each student could walk in a certain way while the rest of the class guess which verb would be most appropriate.

Example 5 Vocabulary exercise from *Advanced English Practice* (OUP)

Complete the sentences, using the words given at the head of the exercise. Use each word *once* only.

stagger	plod	march	pace
loiter	stride	stray	strut
ramble	lurk	creep	wander

1 The victorious army . . . through the conquered city. (soldiers)
2 Not wishing to be discovered, the small boy . . . downstairs. (fear of making a noise)
3 The thieves . . . in the shadows for their unsuspecting victim. (waiting with evil intentions)
4 The turkey . . . up and down the farmyard. (arrogance)
5 The drunkard . . . from the public house and clung to a lamppost. (unsteady movement)

6 We reached the village after a very long walk, and . . . wearily to our hotel. (wearily)
7 The manager . . . into the office and asked who was responsible for the error. (purposeful)
8 The mother told her son to do the errand quickly, and not to . . . on the way. (necessity for speed)
9 The dog had . . . from its home, and was now completely lost. (lose the way)
10 As last Sunday was a fine day, we decided to . . . around the countryside. (walking for pleasure, and without aim)
11 The man whose wife was expecting a child . . . nervously up and down the hospital waiting-room. (nervously up and down)
12 On my first visit to the city, I . . . from place to place without any sense of direction. (no sense of direction)

Enactment, with or without words, becomes all the more effective when there is a framework or context for the lexical items. Take vocabulary to do with cars and driving, for example. Rather than simply providing a list of relevant terms and actions, the teacher can elicit vocabulary by pretending not to know how to drive a car and prompting accordingly. The next stage is to get students in pairs and to ask one of them to give instructions and the others to mime. A chair can be used as the car seat. A similar idea is to combine lexical items into a framework such as a mimed story or song. Let us suppose the words in question are still related to cars and driving. The teacher could sit on a chair and make appropriate mimed gestures for the following episode.

'I was driving home one evening when it began to rain, so I put on the windscreen-wipers and leant forward to try and see more clearly. I wanted to turn left and so I indicated and slowed down. An old woman stepped out in front of me. I put on my brakes and blew the horn loudly. She didn't move. I got out of the car to talk to her and then I noticed my indicator wasn't working. It was my fault!'

The aim is for the students to master the story and use the vocabulary included. Here is how it could be done:

- The teacher tells the episode with the appropriate mime.
- The teacher retells the episode, this time pausing at the mimed gestures for the students to supply the words.
- Then the teacher only mimes and the students supply the words.
- The students try to reconstruct the whole episode with words and mime in small groups.

This technique can be used with any group of words strung into a short story. Its effectiveness stems from the fact that students are unaware how often they are hearing the model or of the fact that they are memorising vocabulary, for their attention is inevitably on the mime.

Lexical items such as phrasal verbs or prepositional phrases are often dealt with in groups for language teaching purposes.

Presentation of the items in Example 6 is done by means of a text on unemployment. After the necessary controlled practice the teacher could approach a freer practice activity as in Activity 14.

Activity 14 Situations
Purpose
Practice of verbs with gerunds
Method
1 The students are paired off and each pair is given a cue card on which is written a situation containing one of the gerunds, eg 'One of you is fed up with doing all the housework all the time.'
2 The students are asked to prepare a short scene to show their situation but without using the actual words on the card.

Example 6 List of verbs followed by the gerund from *Streamline English Destinations*, Unit 5 (OUP)

Teaching points
Verb + -ing form (1)

I enjoy	doing it	I'm afraid of	doing it.
love		terrified of	
like		frightened of	
don't like		scared of	
dislike		tired of	
can't stand		bored with	
hate		fed up with	
		interested in	

I began doing it.
started
stopped
gave up

---

3 The students show their mini-scenes to each other. Afterwards the spectators guess what the words on the card were.

Duration
The students should be given a tight time-limit, say 3-4 minutes, to concentrate their minds. In all, the activity may take 15 minutes.

Sketches and plays are of course a fertile source of active and passive vocabulary. Sketches lend themselves to presentation, activation or reinforcement of lexical items (and structures) because of the repetition and possible memorisation involved (see 4.3 for ways of handling scripts). Hulton (1986) advocates the teacher incorporating vocabulary used in the class into sketches for the enjoyable form of revision such work can provide.

However, not all vocabulary need or indeed should be activated in this way. Students need to acquire a good deal of receptive vocabulary also. Mention has already been made about the involving nature of dramatic dialogue (2.4) and scripts can offer a rich source for vocabulary exploitation. The following plan shows how this could be done using the excerpt in Example 7 taken from a play about a sculptor paralysed from the neck down in an accident.

Aim
   Development of receptive vocabulary
Level
   Advanced
Method
1 The students read through the excerpt silently.
2 Global comprehension questions:
   ● What is Mrs B's job?
   ● How does Ken react to her?
   ● Why?
3 The students try to work out lexical items from their context or their internal features:
   hedge (l.6)
   occupational therapy (l.12)
   cue (l.25)
   appalling (l.29)
   detached (l.32)
4 The students paraphrase expressions:
   I cannot settle for that (l.10)
   Try not to dwell on it (l.11)
   Detach yourself (l.34)
   you turn your (professional) cheek (l.39)

bugger off (l.41)
how does that grab you? (l.44).

Subsequent work on the script (such as playreading) will serve to deepen understanding and retention. (For further information about teaching vocabulary see Wallace [1982]; playreading is dealt with in 4.3.)

Example 7 Extract from the play *Whose Life is it Anyway?* by B. Clark

	MRS B	It's not unusual you know for people injured as you have been to suffer with this depression for a considerable time before they begin to see that a life is possible.
	KEN	How long?
5	MRS B	It varies.
	KEN	Don't **hedge**.
	MRS B	It could be a year or so.
	KEN	And it could last for the rest of my life.
	MRS B	That would be most unlikely.
10	KEN	I'm sorry, but *I cannot settle for that.*
	MRS B	*Try not to dwell on it.* I'll see what I can do to get you started on some **occupational therapy.** Perhaps we could make a start on the reading machines.
	KEN	Do you have many books for those machines?
15	MRS B	Quite a few.
	KEN	Can I make a request for the first one?
	MRS B	If you like.
	KEN	'How to be a sculptor with no hands.'
	MRS B	I'll be back tomorrow with the machine.
20	KEN	It's marvellous, you know.
	MRS B	What is?
	KEN	All you people have the same technique. When I say something really awkward you just pretend I haven't said anything at all. You're all the bloody same . . . Well,
25		there's another outburst. That should be your **cue** to comment on the lightshade or the colour of the walls.

	MRS B	I'm sorry if I have upset you.
	KEN	Of course you have upset me. You and the doctors with your **appalling** so-called professionalism, which is nothing more than a series of verbal tricks to prevent you relating to your patients as human beings.
30		
	MRS B	You must understand; we have to remain relatively **detached** in order to help . . .
35	KEN	That's all right with me. *Detach yourself.* Tear yourself off on the dotted line that divides the woman from the social worker and post yourself off to another patient.
	MRS B	You're very upset . . .
40	KEN	Christ Almighty, you're doing it again. Listen to yourself, woman. I say something offensive about you and *you turn your professional cheek.* If you were human, if you were treating me as human, you'd tell me to *bugger off.* Can't you see that this is why I've decided that life isn't worth living. I am not human, and I'm even more convinced of that by your visit than I was before, so *how does that grab you?* The very exercise of your so-called professionalism makes me want to die. .
45		

3.2 Structures

Much of what is contained in the preceding section applies to the exploitation of structures in language teaching – in particular the use of drama exercises and mime for practice and reinforcement and the benefit of contextualisation that sketches provide.

The application of drama exercises and mime to structures is primarily for activation purposes and supposes that the presentation stage has already been done. With a little imagination there is virtually no structure that cannot be brought to life, with the enhanced mental and physical involvement of the students. Activity 5 (Guess the situation) can be easily adapted to provide simple but enjoyable practice of the present continuous for groups or the whole class, offering relief from grammar exercises and drilling. It also provides a natural context for a structure that is often used artificially in the classroom (I'm walking across the classroom. Now I'm turning on the light', etc). Suitable prompts would be: 'You're eating a banana/reading a newspaper/having a shower/writing a letter/playing table-tennis'. The teacher should elicit as many guesses as possible for the students to gain maximum benefit from the activity. The students may also suggest their own prompts.

Activity 13 (Circulating mime) can also be adapted to practise the present perfect. Again, the guessing element, this time in pairs, makes the activity involving and enjoyable. Suggested prompts are: I've eaten too much/just seen a ghost/passed my driving test/just run a marathon/had a car crash'. The activity can serve as a lead-in to further work on the present perfect by getting the students to write their guesses on the board. These can then be exploited by correcting any errors and rubbing out the verbs in each sentence for student recall and memorisation.

In addition to mime, verbal looseners and sensitivity exercises (see 2.1) can be utilised for structural practice. Activity 15 requires concentration to be done properly. For both actors and students it can be an ensemble-building activity, but in language terms it is an alternative and less monotonous form of drilling.

Activity 15 Speak and mime chain
Purpose
 To practise the past continuous
Method
1 The students should preferably be sitting in a circle or circles. Student A states, or invents, what she was doing

the previous evening at 8 o'clock. She also makes an accompanying mimed gesture.

2 Student B repeats student A's sentence and mime and adds one of his own.
3 Student C repeats the sentences and mimed gestures of student A and then student B before adding her own. The pattern is repeated round the circle.

Example

A: At 8.00 last night I was eating dinner. *(mimes)*
B: At 8.00 last night she was eating dinner *(mimes)* and I was watching TV. *(mimes)*
C: At 8.00 last night she was eating dinner *(mimes)*, he was watching TV *(mimes)*, and I was having a bath. *(mimes)*

Duration

About 7 minutes

Structures can be practised not only through adapting drama exercises in this way but also through sketches specially written for the purpose. The best known ones are those produced by The English Teaching Theatre, and the extract in Example 8 is taken from one of their sketches. Such sketches lend themselves not only to conventional exploitation such as listening practice, gap-filling exercises and pronunciation practice but also to such dramatic activities as enactment, playreading and performances based on parallel situations. There is a more general discussion of how to approach scripts in Chapter 4: here we are concerned with the practice of structural patterns.

Example 8 Extract from 'The Superlative Vacuum-Cleaner'

The salesman goes into the house and closes the door. The housewife rings the bell. The salesman opens the door.

SALESMAN Not today, thank you.
He closes the door. The housewife rings the bell again. The salesman opens the door again, and speaks in a high voice.
Yes?
HOUSEWIFE Hello!
SALESMAN Hello.
HOUSEWIFE My goodness me, what a beautiful house you've got!
SALESMAN Ooh, do you like it?
HOUSEWIFE Like it? It's the most beautiful house I've seen for a long time.
SALESMAN Thank you very much.
HOUSEWIFE May I come in?
SALESMAN Er . . .
HOUSEWIFE Thank you. Oh, what a colourful carpet!
SALESMAN Yes, it's lovely, isn't it?
HOUSEWIFE It's the most colourful carpet I've seen for ages. I should think it was very expensive.
SALESMAN The most expensive one in the shop.
HOUSEWIFE And I suppose you've got a very good vacuum-cleaner to look after it.
SALESMAN A vacuum-cleaner? No, I haven't.
HOUSEWIFE You haven't got a vacuum-cleaner?
SALESMAN No.
HOUSEWIFE Well, madam, this is your lucky day, because I have *here* the best vacuum-cleaner that money can buy: the Superlative vacuum-cleaner.
SALESMAN Is it really good?
HOUSEWIFE Good? Good? It's the . . . the . . .
SALESMAN *(In his own voice:)* Quickest.
HOUSEWIFE . . . the quickest, the . . .
SALESMAN Cleanest.
HOUSEWIFE . . . the cleanest, the cheapest, the smallest, the smartest, the most economical, the most effective, the most beautiful, the most revolutionary vacuum-cleaner in the world.
SALESMAN *(In a high voice again:)* Ooh! How much is it?
HOUSEWIFE Just £65 to you, madam.

SALESMAN   I'll buy one.
HOUSEWIFE Good.
SALESMAN   *(In his own voice:)* Er . . . where's the money?
HOUSEWIFE It's in my handbag on the kitchen table.
SALESMAN   Oh, right. *(In the high voice:)* I'll just go and get some money.
           He goes to the kitchen to get the money.
HOUSEWIFE Good idea, madam. You've made the right decision.
           The salesman comes back, speaking in his own voice.
SALESMAN   Do you know, you're a fantastic saleswoman.
HOUSEWIFE Ooh!
SALESMAN   You've got a fantastic sales technique.
HOUSEWIFE Do you think so?
SALESMAN   Yes, you've got the best sales technique I've seen all day.
HOUSEWIFE Thank you!
SALESMAN   Thank *you*, madam.
           He leaves and closes the door.
           (Speaking to himself, counting the money:) Ten, twenty, thirty, forty, fifty, sixty, sixty-five. Now *that's* the way to sell a vacuum-cleaner.

Off-stage! D. Case and K. Wilson (Heinemann)

After the initial presentation and reading through, the lesson will have the following stages: (a) familiarisation with the language, (b) enactment, and (c) the students' own creations. Let us look at each stage in more detail.

(a) Familiarisation

Part of the process of familiarisation will be effected through the reading through of the sketch, whether in chorus with the teacher or in pairs, or indeed silently. The next stage is to get students to actively memorise the language. In this case it would be best to pick out the parts of the sketch containing the superlatives, for the sketch as a whole would be too big a burden. In order to aid the students' memorisation it is necessary to give them prompts of some sort, and the simplest and most effective way of doing this is to use the blackboard. Cue cards are also possible but these can be cumbersome, distract attention or used to hide behind. With the use of key words, a few prompts suffice to establish the basis of the sketch and these are then practised by the class in the form of a drill.

Example 9 Specimen blackboard plan for sketch prompts

Housewife	*Salesman*
house/beautiful	like it?
come in?	
carpet/colourful	expensive/shop
vacuum-cleaner?	haven't
Superlative vacuum-cleaner	
quick, clean, cheap, small, smart,	
economical, effective, beautiful,	
revolutionary	how much?

(b) Enactment

Having memorised the core of the sketch, the students are ready to act it out. They should be able to improvise or flesh out the other parts and the teacher should make this clear beforehand, preferably by acting out the sketch with a volunteer in front of the class. The easiest way to get the whole class involved is to tell half the class to go to one end of the room and wait. The other half are then spaced around the room and told to imagine they are standing in front of a house (they are the salesman). The group representing the housewife then pair off with a salesman and perform the sales pitch.

Afterwards the roles will need to be reversed in order for all the students to practise the superlatives the housewife uses. With a change of partner, however, something of the original freshness can be retained. The only props needed in the sketch, the vacuum-cleaner and money, can be mimed. To add an extra element, however, students could use paper for the money and a box to represent the cleaner.

(c) The students' creations

The students can now be encouraged to create their own short sketches based on a parallel situation, for example a car salesman trying to convince someone with an old car to buy a new, expensive one. Younger learners would enjoy a more fanciful situation such as a robot or spaceship salesman. Again, because the focus of the lesson is on the use of the superlative, the teacher might ask the students to concentrate on the description by the salesman and to write down some of the sentences he might say. Then the teacher could ask the students to work in pairs and to think of a possible beginning and end to their sketches. After four or five minutes the students should be asked to stand up and run through their whole sketch, preferably exchanging roles after the first time. The teacher can then ask for volunteers to show their sketch to the rest of the class.

This method of practising a structure has several advantages. Firstly, it provides constant repetition and practice of the structure in context, making the language more meaningful and memorable. Secondly, it leads students to memorise key patterns not as an end in itself but as part of the process of enactment. Thirdly, it allows students to make use of their own creativity, both in terms of their physical interpretation of their part and in their invention of a new sketch.

3.3 Dialogues

Open any modern language coursebook and you are sure to find many dialogues. This is unsurprising since it is obviously 'the type of text best suited to . . . teaching the spoken language'. (Byrne: 1976,21) Drama too draws heavily on the use of dialogue, often in extended form. When actors rehearse plays, it is common for the script to be broken down into manageable dialogues, sometimes no longer than those contained in coursebooks, for more intensive work. This will consist of an examination and analysis of the language and meaning followed by experiments with different interpretations of the scene. The way this is handled depends upon the director concerned but the usual methods are either to ask the actors to act out the scene with or without the script (depending on whether they know the lines or not) or to get the actors to improvise the scene in their own words but retaining the essence of the situation and the characters involved. A dramatic interpretation of a dialogue can do much to enliven what might otherwise be flat and mundane and this section aims to show how this can be done. Although there is a difference between dialogues and scripts not only in terms of length but also in nature (dialogues are written primarily for language practice whereas scripts concentrate more on the dramatic element), there is much in the section on handling scripts (4.3) that is of relevance here also.

Most teachers are familiar with the technique of getting students to act out a coursebook dialogue as in Example 10.

Example 10 Typical coursebook dialogue from *New Dimensions* (Macmillan)

> CLERK   Yes, can I help you?
> CUSTOMER   Yes, I'd like to change some travellers' cheques.

CLERK	Of course. What currency have you got?
CUSTOMER	American dollars.
CLERK	The exchange rate is $1.25 to the pound. How much would you like to change?
CUSTOMER	$125.
CLERK	That's £100. How would you like the money?
CUSTOMER	Four twenties, two tens please.
CLERK	Fine, twenty, forty, sixty, eighty, ninety, one hundred. Here's your receipt.
CUSTOMER	Thank you.

The teacher's lesson might be planned as follows:

1 Presentation of the dialogue
2 Pronunciation practice
3 Memorisation
4 Acting out the dialogue in pairs
5 Volunteers' performance before the rest of the class
6 Follow-up.

Ways of handling the memorisation stage have been briefly discussed in section 3.2 where emphasis was put on the use of blackboard cues. Apart from choral repetition, there are other techniques that can be used to wean students away from the text. Probably the most effective is to get the students to look straight at the person they are talking to, a technique known as 'read and look up'. This entails students reading their next sentence, fixing it in their mind, then looking up and saying it to their partner. This half-way stage between reading and acting will be familiar to anyone who has watched rehearsals where actors play their parts with scripts held at their sides for ready reference. An alternative is to use a prompter and arrange students in groups of three with two of them trying out the dialogue and the third with the dialogue in front of him. With regular use the groups of three should evolve a smooth rotation whereby each student gets a turn at both roles, thus:

1. Student 1 – Clerk
   Student 2 – Customer
   Student 3 – Prompter
2. (Student 3 hands dialogue to Student 1)
   Student 1 – Prompter
   Student 2 – Clerk
   Student 3 – Customer
3. (Student 1 hands dialogue to Student 2, etc).

This variation on a theme has the merit of introducing a monitoring element to pair practice as well as fostering peer correction, co-operation and self-reliance.

Once the language has been memorised, the teacher will want to get the students to act out the dialogue. To give some sense of realism desks serve as the counter with the customer and the clerk on either side. To arrange this the teacher can simply ask every other student to stand up and stand opposite one of the seated students: those standing are the customers, those seated are the clerks. Props such as a notebook for the travellers' cheques and paper for the money and the receipt would help to make the language meaningful and memorable. 'Here's your receipt' is meaningless without the appropriate gesture. After students have acted out the dialogue, the teacher will get them to repeat it but this time switching roles and preferably partners as well: a change of face will help the student better identify with the change of role.

Valid as the above approach may be, it lacks something in dramatic terms. There is no characterisation and no conflict. These two vital ingredients can be used to good effect in exploiting dialogues for language purposes.

Example 11

A I like your fur coat, Helen.
B Do you?
A Yes, it looks very expensive.
B Really? It wasn't expensive . . . it was second-hand.
A Was it? It doesn't look second-hand, it looks brand-new.

Streamline English Connections, Unit 2 (OUP)

Look at Example 11. The teacher gives student A and student B suggestions as to how they should play their parts. These suggestions are kept unknown to the other person involved. The sort of suggestions that might be used are:

Student A
- You don't like Helen.

- You've got a cold.

- You're rather deaf.

Student B
- You're in a hurry.

- You're very proud of your coat.

- You're feeling depressed.

This technique can be used either in pair work or as a whole class activity but both rely upon an element of guessing. For pair work the teacher should separate the class into two, sending them to opposite ends of the room or sending one half outside if practicable. The teacher then whispers the suggestion to each group in turn, making sure the other group do not hear. Alternatively, the teacher can show each group a piece of paper on which the suggestion is written. The two groups then pair off and act out the dialogue in keeping with the suggestion. Afterwards the teacher asks members of each group to guess what the other was attempting to portray. Roles are then reversed and new suggestions given. For the whole class activity the basic idea is the same but this time two students act out their dialogues in front of the rest of the class who try to guess the suggestions given to both participants. This would only be suitable for groups that were familiar with each other and with the idea of acting, since the performance involved would be embarrassing to some.

Another element of dramatic interpretation that can be used for dialogue exploitation is that of improvisation. For actors improvisation is a means of experimenting with characterisation; for students improvisation allows them to experiment with the language. With short dialogues such as in Example 11 students can be asked to improvise continuations in the following manner:

1 The students memorise the dialogue.
2 The students act out the dialogue in pairs.
3 The students act out the dialogue again but this time continue in their own words. If necessary, the teacher provides a prompt such as: 'Student A – comment on Helen's other clothes.'
4 The students 'polish' (improve and perfect) their improvisations. (Monitor sheets can be used to good effect at this stage. See Norrish [1983] in this series.)
5 Volunteers show their versions to the rest of the class. Alternatively, versions are recorded and the language monitored during the playback session.

The benefit of this approach is that students repeat the original dialogue several times without being aware of it since the focus switches to the continuation. It also exposes students to the real world of uncharted language as they move from the security of the known (textbook dialogue) to the insecurity of the unknown (improvisation). Furthermore, if the improvisation is properly directed, it will allow students further practice in the sort of language use being presented in the original dialogue. A further possibility is to get students to improvise a parallel situation so that the language items are recycled but not repeated verbatim. In the case of the above dialogue, the second-hand fur coat could be replaced by a jacket bought in a sale, with the teacher dividing the class and giving each group separate instructions:

Student A
Your friend has a smart jacket which looks new and expensive.

Student B
You bought your jacket very cheaply in a sale.

The teacher then tells the two groups to pair off and to continue a conversation for as long as they can.

3.4 Free stage

The preceding sections have dealt with controlled language practice for the most part. However, students also need to be given the opportunity to try out the newly learnt language in situations that approximate to real life and in which they are free to choose how to formulate what they want to say. The teacher's task is to create a suitable framework that suggests rather than dictates the use of the language presented and practised earlier in the lesson. Drama activities can be an enormous help to the teacher in the creation of this free stage, for drama is essentially about the simulation of real-life and the 're-creating' of reality. True drama does not merely hold up a mirror to reality, however, it tries to capture something of significance in the portrayal as well as holding attention and interest. By borrowing from the world of drama, teachers can breathe life into what may otherwise be arid or academic exercises.

To give an illustration of what is meant by the above, compare the two scenarios in Example 12 in which pairs of students are practising ways of asking for information (see also 2.3).

Example 12 Two scenarios for comparison of dramatic and language potential

Scenario 1
One student is pretending to be a stranger in town and the other, a resident, is answering questions.
The students are seated at desks.
Both characters follow cues in the textbook, aware of the eventual outcome.

Scenario 2
One student is pretending to be a stranger in town and the other, a resident, is somewhat deaf.
The students are standing in pairs around the room.
A controlled but improvised dialogue is attempted with the students unaware of the eventual outcome.

Whereas the first activity might be quieter and easier to control, it is also likely to be less enjoyable and less likely to involve the students fully and thereby be less effective in the learning process. The second example gains by drawing upon elements of drama, namely the presence of conflict, the imitation of reality and the practice of improvisation. Activity 16 shows how to incorporate such elements into a simple role-play.

Activity 16 Asking for information (role-play)
Aim
  To practise ways of asking for information
Method
1 The teacher divides the class into two: group A and group B. Group A are sent outside the room.
2 The teacher tells group A that they are a stranger in town

and want to find out where the bus station is, how long it takes to get there and when the next bus to London is.
3 The teacher tells group B that they are in their home-town waiting for a bus at a bus-stop and that they have difficulty hearing. The teacher asks group B to spread themselves out around the class and imagine they are waiting for a bus.
4 Before bringing in group A, the teacher tells them they are walking down a street when they see someone waiting at a bus-stop to whom they should direct their questions.
5 The two groups pair off and interact.
6 The teacher compares what happened in various pairs.

Duration

Between 7 and 10 minutes

The use of an objective of which the other participants are unaware is a common technique in drama exercises (and plays) for it adds purpose and tension to what might otherwise be pointless platitudes. The rather limited objectives in the above examples can be taken a step further by setting up a more complex 'objectives role-play' (see Goodfellow: 1982) as in Activity 17.

Activity 17 Objectives role-play

Aim

To practise ways of asking for information

Method

1 Separate students into three groups: group A are travel agents, group B one half of a married couple, and group C the other half.
2 Give groups a preparation task:
   - Group A – to prepare five different package holidays with destination and cost
   - Group B – to decide with one another what sort of holiday

they most want to have. (The group should reach a consensus.)
- Group C – as group B.
3 The three groups are now given their objectives:
- Group A – to sell the customers as expensive a holiday from their selection as they can
- Group B – to get information about what holidays are on offer and to choose the one they most like, regardless of cost, as they need to relax
- Group C – to find out information about the holidays on offer and to choose one they like but which will not cost them more than they can afford.
4 The teacher explains to the class as a whole that the situation takes place in a travel agent's and asks group A to go and stand behind desks (representing counters). The teacher explains that a couple will visit the travel agent's and asks group B and group C to pair off. The couple then approach one of the travel agents.
5 The role-play should now take on its own dynamism as members of each group interact.
6 After a suitable length of time, perhaps when several of the groups have finished, the teacher brings the role-play to a close.
7 The teacher can now *either:*
   (a) find out and compare what happened in the various groups as a whole-class activity, *or*
   (b) ask the students to return to their original groups and compare with other members of their group what happened and how far they succeeded in achieving their objective.

Duration
About 20 minutes

The objectives role-play is highly effective in producing

language because of the tasks involved. Complex as it might seem, it is relatively easy to prepare, requiring the teacher to choose the objectives and methods of organisation. These objectives should be conflicting but not contradictory, for that could lead to an unsatisfactory stalemate. Thus Activity 17 would have less momentum if the objectives were: 'Travel agents – you do not want to sell anything less than £300. Customers – you do not want anything more than £300.'

In the previous examples the teacher provided the situations. An alternative approach is to provide the language and let the students make up the situation themselves. This is done by giving students groups of phrases or sentences containing whatever language is being taught in the lesson. This might consist of a structure such as the present perfect (I haven't finished yet. Look what the postman has brought) or functional components such as those in Example 13.

Example 13 Functional components extracted from *Functions of English* (CUP)

Presentation: complaining

A direct complaint in English often sounds very rude indeed. To be polite we usually 'break it gently' and use expressions like these before we actually come to the point:

I wonder if you could help me . . .
Look, I'm sorry to trouble you, but . . .
I've got a bit of a problem here, you see . . .
I'm sorry to have to say this, but . . .

The students have to prepare a short scene in which the sentences are used in a more or less plausible manner. They should first work in pairs or groups of three to think up a suitable situation and then practise or rehearse it for possible presentation to others. The sort of situations that students might decide upon in the case of complaints are bad service in a shop or restaurant, a rude official, someone being offensive in a train or bus, etc.

To conclude this section, it is worth reiterating the value of drama activities in the free stage. Teachers are concerned to bring the outside world into the classroom so that the language being taught does not simply exist in a vacuum but has relevance to the everyday world. Without some of the skills and techniques developed by those working in the sphere of drama, the free stage can fall flat and lack even the appearance of real life. By getting students to act out situations, introducing an element of conflict or tension and making use of students' creativity, the teacher can help students to activate the language in a stimulating and enjoyable manner. In Chapter 4 there are further activities, some of which may be adapted for the purposes of the free stage.

3.5 Comprehension and interpretation

Actors who are working on a play have to ensure that they have a common understanding of the text. They will probably to do this by open discussion with the director, though there are dictatorial directors who like to impose their interpretation on the group. (In this respect directors have much in common with teachers!) Once the general direction has been agreed, attention will be turned to particular characters or scenes and examined in more detail. At some stage the first experiments with portrayal of the characters will be made and adjustments and alterations to voice and manner made. Then individual scenes will be worked on the process of rehearsals begun. Thus it is that comprehension must precede the art of interpretation, being a means rather than an end in itself.

In the language classroom, comprehension of reading and

listening passages can be handled in different ways. This will depend to a large extent on the nature of the passage and the reason for reading/listening. Certain exercises would be quite inappropriate to certain tasks: it would be unhelpful to students to answer detailed questions on a passage clearly designed to be scanned for information, for example. Information on the variety of types and purposes of comprehension exercises can be found in two other books in this series, namely *Reading in the language classroom* (Williams: 1984) and *Developing Listening Skills* (Rixon: 1986). On most occasions comprehension will best be dealt with in the form of check questions, summaries, charts, graphs, etc described in these two books, but there are occasions when the process of dramatic interpretation described above will be rewarding not only in terms of comprehension but also in educational terms, for it involves active participation, collaborative creativity and is experiential rather than solely cerebral. A simple but effective means of checking comprehension in this way is to make use of a technique (see Example 14) borrowed from Total Physical Response, referred to in 1.3.2, by which students perform or mime the statements in question.

Example 14 Using a method based on Total Physical Response

You're shopping.
Go into a shop.
Look at some coats.
Try on a red one.
Look in the mirror.
It's too small. Take it off.
Try on a blue one.
Look in the mirror.

It's too big. Take it off.
Try on a yellow one.
Look in the mirror.
It fits.
You like it.
Take it off.
Pay the assistant.
Go out of the shop.

You can use a box of cuisenaire rods or coloured paper as the coats. This helps the students visualise colour and size better.

Using the second series of commands as the basis for your lesson, you can then conduct the lesson following the sequence that the TPR manuals suggest.

1. You give the command while you or a good student serves as the model.
2. Then you ask the students to carry out the commands as you give them.
3. Then give the students the text to study the vocabulary.
4. In small groups or pairs, the students ask each other to carry out the commands. (They should try not to use their texts. You may put word cues on the board.)

'Using Total Physical Response Communicatively',
T. Tomscha in *Practical English Teaching*, Sept 1984

Example 15 A comprehension passage from *Kernel Intermediate* (Longman)

The Man Who Escaped

Episode 5

SYNOPSIS: *Coke escaped from prison and hid in a field. It was very cold and he knew he had to find warm clothes and food somewhere. He saw a house in the country, isolated and far away from the nearest town. He stood outside the house before going in. He could not understand why there was no noise coming from it, not even the sound of a radio or television.*

1 Coke listened for several seconds but he could not hear anything at all. And yet there was smoke coming from the chimney and there was a light on in the front room! 'Why is it so quiet? Is it a trap? Are the police waiting for me in there?' he asked himself. He went to the front door and pushed it. To his surprise it was open! He went in very quietly. In the front room there was a fire burning in the fireplace. The room was clean, small and very warm. There was very little furniture in it – only a couch and a table in front of the

fire and two old-fashioned chairs. There were also some photographs on the shelf above the fire. They were yellow and old. One of them was a young man in a World War I uniform. There were also a few of the same young man and also a woman in old-fashioned wedding-clothes.

2 Suddenly Coke froze. There was someone else in the room. He knew it. He could feel it! He turned around quickly and, at the same time, put his hand in his pocket. There was a small knife there. He saw an old woman. She had a covered dish in her hands and there was a delicious smell of meat and vegetables coming from it. She did not look afraid. She did not even look surprised.
'I'm sorry,' she said, and put the dish down on the table.
Coke could hardly believe his ears. Here he was, a stranger in her house and yet she said *she* was sorry!

3 'I'm sorry,' she said again. 'I didn't hear you. Did you knock? I'm deaf, you see.' She pointed to her ear, shook her head and said 'deaf' a second time. 'People often come to the door and knock, but I don't hear them. I'm glad you came in.'
Coke stared at her for a second and then finally found his voice. 'I . . . I'm sorry. I just stepped in.'
He looked down at his clothes. His prison uniform was so dirty that it was impossible to tell what kind of uniform it was. Then he suddenly had an idea.
'I'm a mechanic from a garage in town. I came to repair a lorry somewhere out here but the road was icy. I had an accident. I . . . fell off my motorbike.'
He had to say this several times before she finally understood him. When she did, she gave him some hot water and soap and afterwards some food. The only thing he needed now was a change of clothes!

Not all texts lend themselves to straightforward treatment. However, it is usually possible to make use of action or acting to clarify comprehension. Here is how this would work with Example 15.

1 Global comprehension: the students read or listen to the whole passage to get the overall meaning.
2 The students are asked to picture the scene in their minds (Who is standing where? How do they look? What are they doing? etc) as they listen or read again.
3 The class is divided down the middle into two halves. Group A are told they will take the part of the old woman, group B that of Coke. The class reads or listens once more, taking notes.
4 The students are allowed a few minutes to compare ideas with their neighbours.
5 The students from the two groups are paired off and told to improvise the scene between the old woman and Coke.
6 The students are asked to polish their improvisations.
7 Volunteers show their interpretations to the rest of the class.

Though this approach requires the students to study the text carefully, it also makes demands on the students' willingness to pretend and to play the part. For classes unused to drama activities, use can be made of the interview strategy. After the initial comprehension work on the passage, students would be divided into two groups, one to play the part of the old woman and the other to take the part of a policeman. The first group would be asked to read through the text paying particular attention to what the old woman did, while the second group would formulate questions to put to the old woman. To avoid a routine question-and-answer exercise the teacher could encourage the groups to think about characterisation: that of the old woman is suggested in the text, that of the policeman could be decided by the teacher or group. Students then pair off and act out the interview, or write out the dialogue first and then use it as a model for acting out. This 'extract and write' technique provides useful writing work as well as developing accuracy. Afterwards the students could discuss and compare what happened in the various pairs. The groups could then be reformed and another interview set up, this time between Coke and a journalist.

In the passage in Example 15 there is already some dialogue contained in the text. This is not always the case, but absence of dialogue need not affect the basic technique of getting students to take on the roles of the characters concerned. Interpretations of texts do not have to be spoken, either. Group preparation of a mime based on a written or spoken story can involve the same degree of comprehension and interaction. Not all texts will lend themselves to exploitation through drama activities, but their use can introduce an extra dimension of student involvement and interpretation.

3.6 A sample lesson

As both teacher and students become used to drama activities, opportunities for their use will be found on an increasing number of occasions. Some coursebooks have springboards for drama activities built into them but even the drier ones that concentrate on language analysis can be enlivened by a teacher with some imagination. In this section the book under scrutiny is *Kernel Plus* (O'Neill: 1972). It is a book that has been and still is widely used around the world. It is eclectic in approach with a variety of skills practised in each unit. From the point of view of drama activities it has considerable potential for exploitation. The following suggestions are all based on the first unit.

The course begins with the page reproduced in Example 16. The intention is evidently to stimulate student practice of the present simple and continuous in a meaningful context. Even

Example 16

Unit 1, Lesson 1

Traffic in our cities

1

This is a traffic jam. Most of these people are trying to get to work. They all work in the city but few of them live there. They are feeling very angry and frustrated at the moment because the traffic is hardly moving. Traffic jams like this happen every day. The problem is getting worse, all the time.

Paired Practice

Imagine you are a reporter. You are interviewing some of the drivers in this traffic jam. What questions do you ask? Give the answers as well! You want to know:
1 where they are going
2 where they work
3 where they live
4 how they are feeling at the moment
5 why
6 how often these jams happen
7 if things are getting better

2

This policeman is directing traffic in the centre of London. He does this every day. He often suffers from headaches. He simply does not get enough oxygen.

Questions

Ask the policeman:
1 what he is doing
2 if he does this every day
3 why he suffers from headaches
Give the answers as well.

3

Professor Colin Campbell is a famous traffic expert. He believes that most of our cities are dying. "Most of our cities are being destroyed by the motor car," he is saying. At the moment he is being interviewed on television.

Questions
a
1 Who is this man?
2 What does he believe?
3 What is happening at the moment?
b
Now interview him yourself. Ask:
1 What is happening to our cities
2 What they are being destroyed by

Kernel Plus (Longman)

Example 17

Unit 1, Lesson 1

Grammar Exposition and Exercise

> What causes headaches?
> What does the policeman suffer from?

1a

Imagine you are interviewing the policeman. Notice the two different question constructions.

> You know that *something causes his headaches.*
> You ask, "What causes your headaches?"
> You know that *he suffers from something.*
> You ask, "What do you suffer from?"

1b

Comment
1 If *what* or *who* is the subject, the *doer of the action,* do *not* use the question auxiliary (*do, does, did*).
2 But use the auxiliary if *what* or *who* is the object and if you are using a *full verb* (not *be* or any of the modals like *can, should, must, ought to,* etc.)

1c

Now ask the policeman questions with *who* or *what.*
You know that:
1 something gives him headaches
2 someone uses the road every day
3 something happens every morning
4 he does something every day
5 someone helps him when there is a traffic jam

6 he wears something when it rains
7 he does something when there is an accident

1d

Transfer
You are also interviewing a motorist. Ask various questions beginning with *who, what, what sort of,* etc. Ask:

1 what sort of petrol he uses
2 what sort of car he drives
3 who (if anybody) travels with him every morning
4 what gives him the most trouble with his car
5 who he hates most, traffic policemen or other motorists
6 what causes the traffic jam

Think of more questions you might ask about the cost, how crowded the roads are, which roads he uses to get to work, what he does when he is in a traffic jam, etc.

> How many children use this road?
> How many children does Mrs Clay know?

2a

Comment
the same rule applies to *how much* and *how many*.
When they go with the subject the question auxiliary is not used.

2b

Now ask the motorist questions with *how much* or *how many*. You know that:

1 other motorists use the same road
2 accidents happen on the road every day
3 he sees accidents every week
4 he knows other motorists
5 his car uses petrol
6 he spends money on his car
7 Super X Petrol costs money
8 other motorists use Super X Petrol

Kernel Plus (Longman)

Example 18

Unit 1, Lesson 2

Dialogue/Practice

Listen to the dialogue on tape. Then use this skeleton to reproduce what Linda said.

1

Dialogue
On the 79
CONDUCTOR: Fares, please. Any more fares?
LINDA: . . . .
CONDUCTOR: Your'e on the wrong bus. We don't go to Marble Arch.
LINDA: . . . . you? I thought . . . .
CONDUCTOR: No. This is a 79. You want a 79A.
LINDA: . . . ? Where . . . . one?
CONDUCTOR: Get off at the next stop.
Waiting at the stop
LINDA: . . . . me . . . . know . . . . the 79A . . . . here?
WOMAN: The 79A? No, it stops up the road.
LINDA: But a conductor told me . . . . here.
WOMAN: Oh, dear. They don't know what they're talking about. Where d'you want to go, then?
LINDA: Marble Arch. And . . . . much time . . . .
WOMAN: Marble Arch? You want an 89B, then. Look! One's coming now!
On the 89B
CONDUCTOR: Fares please.
LINDA: . . . . please. Uh, you *do* . . . . Marble Arch, ... ?
CONDUCTOR: That's right. Four please.
LINDA: How long . . . . to get there?
CONDUCTOR: Oh, it takes about half an hour this time of the day.
LINDA: . . . .? But . . . . only a mile . . . .
CONDUCTOR: Yes, but it's all traffic. If you're in a hurry, you ought to take the Underground or walk. It's much faster!

Practice

2a

Listen carefully to Linda's intonation here.

> CONDUCTOR: **We don't go to Marble Arch.**
> LINDA: **Don't you? I thought you did.**

Answer these statements in the same way.
1 These buses don't go to Marble Arch.
2 That isn't the right fare.
3 Those aren't English pennies.
4 This bus doesn't stop here.
5 You aren't on the right bus.
6 You don't know how to do this exercise

2b

Linda did not say to the woman at the stop:

> **"Does the 79A stop here?" Instead she said:**
> **"Excuse me. Do you know if the 79A stops here?"**

Ask these questions in the same way.
1 Does this bus go to Marble Arch?
2 Is it 10 o'clock yet?
3 How often does the 79A run?
4 Do other buses go to Marble Arch.
5 Is Marble Arch near here?

3

Transfer
You are at a railway station in London. You want to go to York (a city in Yorkshire). You want to know when the next train leaves, if there is a dining car on the train, etc. Think of all the questions you might ask. What exactly would you say?

Kernel Plus (Longman)

so there is a danger that the exercises will not fully involve the students, remaining fixed as it were on the printed page and forgotten with the turning of the page. The exercises can be made to affect the students more directly in the following way.

Aim

Presentation, comprehension and exploitation of 'Traffic in our cities', Unit 1, *Kernel Plus*

Method

Presentation (12 minutes):

1 The teacher places 3 chairs in front of the class and asks 3 volunteers to sit on them (to represent 3 commuters, each driving a car).
2 The teacher places another 2 chairs in front and facing each other and asks for more volunteers (to represent the professor and the interviewer).
3 The teacher asks for another volunteer and arranges the student in the pose of a policeman directing traffic.
4 The teacher reads aloud the three passages and points to the appropriate students (the students' books are closed).
5 The teacher checks comprehension using the volunteers as the focus of questions:

commuters
- Who are these people?
- Where are they going?
- How are they feeling?
- Why?
- Is the problem getting better or worse?

policeman
- Who is this person?
- What is he doing?
- How often does he do it?
- How does he feel?
- Why?

professor ⎫ Who are these two people?
and ⎬ What is happening at the moment?
interviewer ⎭ What does the professor believe?

Development (15 minutes):
1 The students open their books: volunteers digest information about their roles, the rest of the class prepare a question each to ask the characters.
2 The teacher checks that volunteers understand their roles and checks the questions of the rest of the class.
3 The students close their books. The teacher introduces a television programme on traffic in the cities with a live audience invited to put questions to people affected by traffic problems.
4 The teacher chairs the question session.

The impersonation of the characters concerned not only brings the activity to life but it also engages students in communication that is more interesting and real than a straightforward textbook exercise. The same basic strategy underlies the handling of the grammar follow-up (see Example 17). Such grammar exercises can be tedious and off-putting to many students. Activities 18, 19 and 20 present ways in which the exercises concerned in Example 17 can be fully exploited *and* enjoyable.

Activity 18 Acting in character
Purpose
   Exploitation of Exercise 1c, Unit 1, *Kernel Plus:* practice of questions with *who* or *what*
Method
1 The students prepare all 7 questions in Exercise 1c.
2 The teacher takes 3 students outside and tells them that they are to play the policeman. One of them is to be very polite, one aggressive and one forgetful.

3 The teacher and policemen re-enter and the teacher invites the class to put the 7 questions to each of the policemen (in other words, 21 questions in all.)
4 The teacher then asks the class to guess the sort of mood or character of the policemen.

Duration:
At least 10 minutes, including the initial preparation

Activity 18 allows the students to hear the seven questions three times without any sense of monotony, for the attention will inevitably be on the policemen and the different and unexpected ways in which they reply. The activity provides a missing element in this respect, for the exercise as it stands has no information gap – the students all know the answers to the questions, since they are contained in the text or are a matter of common sense. The guessing element substitutes for the information gap and thus ensures that the exercise is less mechanical. In Activity 19 the extra element that the drama activity introduces is a sense of conflict.

Activity 19 Objectives
Purpose
Exploitation of Exercise 1d, Unit 1, *Kernel Plus:* practice of *wh-* questions

Method
1 The students work out the 6 questions in Exercise 1d.
2 The class is divided into two. Group A shut their books and help each other to try and remember all 6 questions. Group B decide possible answers to the questions.
3 The teacher shows group A a piece of paper on which is written: 'You work for a bicycle manufacturer. You want the government to ban cars from cities. Try not to tell this to the motorists.'
4 The teacher shows the motorists a piece of paper on which

is written: 'You're in a bad mood because of the traffic jams. However, answer the questions you are asked. See if you can find out why the other person is asking you the questions.'
5 Students from the two groups pair off and the questions are put.
6 The teacher finds out what happened in the various pairs, asking the student from group A about the attitude of the motorist and the student from group B the reason for the questions. (In a class used to such activities at least several members of group A will have made up imaginative lies.)

Duration
About 10 minutes

The framework provided by Activity 19 is one which is more likely to involve the students than the simple interview suggested by the textbook. The actual questions and answers are unlikely to have much intrinsic interest in themselves and the objectives compensate for this. In Activity 20 it is the sketch-like nature that provides the compensating factor.

Activity 20 Argumentative couple
Purpose
   Exploitation of Exercise 2b, Unit 1, *Kernel Plus:* practice of questions with *how much* and *how many*
Method
1 The students prepare the 8 questions in pairs.
2 One third of the class leaves the room with their books.
3 The teacher tells those remaining to choose a partner. They are to be a couple/good friends who share a car. They can never agree about anything and always contradict each other. The teacher can briefly demonstrate with one pair.
4 The teacher tells the group outside that they are going to put the questions to a couple and that they should try to

remember the answers so as to report them afterwards.
5 The interviewers choose a couple and put their questions.
6 Afterwards the teacher asks the interviewers to report back (if they can!).

Duration
Between 10 and 15 minutes

However noisy the last activity may be, a lot of valuable language practice will be going on, not only in terms of the controlled questioning but also in the students' improvised answers. In addition, the students' enjoyment of the activity is likely to make them look favourably on the grammar exercises that will recur in every unit of the book.

The presentation and practice stages of Unit One are accompanied by reading and listening passages. There is also a fairly lengthy dialogue in each unit, that of Unit One being reproduced in Example 18. Sometimes the dialogues lend themselves to the treatment described earlier in 3.2 where key sentences are picked out for memorisation and acting out. In this case acting out the dialogue as it stands could be cumbersome and ineffective, because of the difficulty of Linda getting on and off buses with any credibility. One way to approach it is given in Activity 21, whereby the gradual building up of very short scenes prepares students for the acting out of a whole scene at the end.

Activity 21 Enactment
Purpose
Practice and reinforcement of the dialogue in Unit 1, *Kernel Plus*, in particular the question-forms involved.
Method
1 The students listen to the dialogue on the tape and the teacher checks that they are sure of the missing words.
2 The teacher practises the pronunciation of the first part between the conductor and Linda. The teacher asks the

students to shut their books and then elicits the salient sentences. When the students seem able to recall the dialogue readily enough, the teacher asks every other student to stand up and move to the front of the class.

3 The teacher tells those that are sitting to play the part of Linda and those that are standing to go up to Linda and begin the dialogue with 'Fares, please.'

4 The teacher asks the students to change roles and partners. This time they should concentrate on the portrayal of the two characters. What sort of person might the conductor be? How might he feel? How might Linda feel? (Such questions help the students to give a little bit more to the repetition, which otherwise might seem perfunctory.)

5 The teacher deals with the second and third part of the dialogue in a similar manner.

6 The teacher now sets the students to work on a parallel situation, in this case a person travelling on the wrong train. The students work in groups of three: a Linda-equivalent, a passenger on the train and a ticket-collector. The teacher outlines the situation: Linda is travelling on a train and is worried it might not be the right one. She asks the other passenger, who tells her she's on the wrong train. Then the ticket-collector comes along. He gives her all the information she needs to get to her destination.

7 The teacher suggests the physical shape of the scene (two chairs opposite each other to suggest passengers in a train). The teacher then tells the students to improvise the scene. Afterwards the groups should polish their improvisations, then one or two be invited to perform to the rest of the class.

8 The teacher takes up language items in the students' scenes for praise, correction or further practice.

Duration

A whole period of 40–50 minutes

Points for consideration:
- the effectiveness of mime in reinforcing vocabulary and structure.
- the value of acting out in vocabulary teaching
- the use of play scripts for developing receptive vocabulary
- the value of sketches for reinforcing vocabulary and structure
- ways of injecting life into dialogues through the addition of character and conflict
- the benefit of improvising the continuation of a dialogue
- the use of acting out and role-play as aids to comprehension
- the value of drama activities in the free stage
- the application of drama activities to coursebook material.

4 Drama-based lessons with a script

4.1 Working with scripts

Reference has already been made to the linguistic and psychological benefits of using a script (2.4). In addition, much of what was said in the sections dealing with the exploitation of short sketches for specific language purposes such as vocabulary (3.1) and structural practice (3.2) is of relevance to work on scripts, particularly suggestions for memorisation and improvised enactment. This chapter concentrates on the use of scripts for general language purposes where work on the script is the main focus of the lesson. Not only do such lessons serve language goals such as comprehension, mastering of new items and patterns, and fluency practice but they also meet educational requirements such as developing self-awareness, self-confidence and collaboration. Where work on a script is intended to lead to a school play or public performance of some sort there are other considerations to bear in mind and these are discussed in 4.6

For those unused to drama activities scripts are probably the easiest way forward. They offer a firm foundation to both student and teacher alike. However, paradoxical as it may seem, scripts can prevent rather than promote the cause of drama. This is evident from that all-too-familiar picture of a group of students standing and staring at their scripts while one of them reads aloud quite unintelligibly. There is no spontaneity, no meaningful interaction, no sense of dramatic tension and no communication – in short, little of any value! In the struggle to master words that are alien, the students forget the intention and context of the language and fail in their prime aim of communication. Hence many teachers of drama in L1 situations frown upon the use of script altogether and point to the quicker return and greater opportunity for self-expression in developmental drama (as in the next chapter). This is fine for teachers and students experienced and competent in the use of drama activities and confident of their language ability. However, for the great majority, scripts will be easier to handle than spontaneous activities such as improvisation. Scripts in themselves do not offer any guarantee of success in either drama or language terms. They need to be selected and treated in an appropriate manner if their potential is to be properly exploited. The next two sections concern themselves with these two key factors.

4.2 Choosing a script

An unsuitable script can lead to problems such as indifference to the subject-matter, inability to relate to the characters, not enough parts for the members of the group, technical or acting demands beyond the capabilities of the class or a language level beyond the students' competence. Careful selection, however, should minimise the occurrence of these problems.

4.2.1 Appropriate language and topic

The choice of script will of course be affected by its ultimate purpose. A far wider range of texts will be found to be suitable for the purposes of playreading than for public performance, for example. Whatever the purpose, the language involved must be accessible to the students and relevant to their needs: dialect and historial language are unlikely to be of value. As well as the type of level of language, the theme of the play is also a vital consideration, for unless it arouses interest, the sustained work involved in working on a script will be impossible to achieve satisfactorily.

4.2.2 Number and type of roles

Criteria such as language and topic are of course common to the selection of all language texts. There are, however, one or two considerations that are peculiar to scripts. The first of these concerns the number of roles, since ideally the teacher will be looking to involve the whole class in a more or less equal way. Scripts that rely on one or two main parts with several minor roles are unlikely to engage all the students, for there will inevitably be situations where the majority are passive and uninvolved in the action. It will, however, prove near impossible to find just the number of roles desired on any one occasion. One solution for those scripts with a small number of roles is to divide the class into smaller groups to match the number of parts. Where there is the odd one or two students extra, one member of the group can be appointed director with overall responsibility for the performance of the group. Where the students are very young or inexperienced, an alternative is to look for a particular task that might need doing, such as sound effects, or to suggest the idea of a Master of Ceremonies to introduce and conclude the scenes. There are also occasions where students can play more than one part each because the various characters do not appear in the same scene. On the other hand, a role could be divided between two students by the simple expedient of making, for example, 'Soldier' into 'Soldiers' and dividing the lines accordingly. It is also possible to write in new lines for an extra character or characters, lines that are inessential to the plot in that they do not alter the nature of the play but which allow for all the students in the group to have a part.

Though the gender of the characters can cause concern to some, it need not necessarily be a problem. Sometimes the names can simply be changed to that of the opposite sex. Where this proves impossible, students can take the part of the opposite sex. Those that are reluctant to do so should have it pointed out to them that if they can take the role of a millionaire or a doctor, then they can just as well take the role of a person of the opposite sex. Possible embarrassment can be caused by romantic scenes, particularly with adolescents, and in such cases the casting needs to be done with care. Extroverts might relish the chance to play the opposite sex but overacting and parody can lead to frivolity. Teachers need to exercise caution in this regard.

4.2.3 Length

The length of the script is also crucial. Again the use to which it is to be put is vital to the decision; scripts for playreading purposes can be of much greater length than those designed for acting out. In the latter case it is advisable to under- rather than overestimate the length since the burden of reading out loud and memorising lines in a foreign language are considerable. In this respect it is sometimes worthwhile concentrating on particular scenes in a longer play rather than attempting to deal intensively with the whole of it. This offers considerable scope for the treatment of the script, for the whole play can be read and discussed with reference to the characters and their intentions, which will then be exemplified in the scene concerned. The plays of Oscar Wilde, such as *The*

Importance of Being Earnest and *Lady Windermere's Fan*, lend themselves to treatment of this sort, for whereas they are far too long for language learners to do anything but read them through, there are individual scenes that can be effectively exploited by being acted out (see Example 19). As a general point it is worth remembering that professional actors can spend many hours on the interpretation of just one short passage, and that both for language and dramatic purposes it is best to keep the length of the script to the minimum possible.

4.2.4 Dramatic demands

A final factor in the selection of scripts is that of the dramatic demands inherent in the action. One cannot expect students to be natural actors and the teacher needs to be sensitive to the group's capability when making the selection. Classes that are used to drama activities will be less inhibited than others about performing in front of each other. They will be better able to cope with scenes involving emotion of any sort or scenes where the verbal communication is supplemented by non-linguistic signals and a sub-text (the pauses in Pinter's plays, for example). For classes where acting of this kind seems improbable, it is advisable to choose scripts where the action is on a par with the sort of role-plays that are commonly employed in language work or to make use of the short humorous sketches that rely on play-acting.

While the range of plays and playlets is obviously vast at the advanced and higher intermediate levels where use can be made of authentic scripts, the choice at lower levels is very much more limited. For this reason it is often a viable proposition for the teacher or group to create a sketch and suggestions for this are given in a later section (4.4).

4.3 Handling a script

The handling of scripts is another vital element in determining the outcome of their use in class. While there is no simple format to guarantee success, there are strategies that can help avoid the pitfalls. General adherence to sound teaching principles is the teacher's best maxim in this respect, and much of what is to follow applies equally to other areas of language teaching. In section 2.4 reference was made to the conventional manner of procedure when tackling a script:

---
presentation – discussion – rehearsal – performance.

Before embarking on this process, students' interest in the subject-matter of the script should be aroused. After all, unlike actors, students have no implicit motivation in working on a script. (See Williams [1984] and Rixon [1986] in this series for reading and listening warm-ups.) The simplest way of creating interest is to introduce the situation concerned and ask students what they think might happen. Let us take as an example the famous 'handbag' scene from Oscar Wilde's *The Importance of Being Earnest* in which Lady Bracknell interviews Jack to assess his suitability as a son-in-law (see Example 19).

Example 19 Abridged extract from *The Importance of Being Earnest* by Oscar Wilde

> *Jack has just declared his love to Gwendolen and is in the middle of proposing when her mother, Lady Bracknell enters. Lady Bracknell, sends her daughter out of the room and proceeds to find out about Jack's position and background. Among other things, she wants to know about his income and property:*
>
> JACK: I have a country house with some land, of course, attached to it, about fifteen hundred acres, I believe; but I don't depend on that for my real income.

LADY BRACKNELL: A country house! How many bedrooms? Well, that point can be cleared up afterwards. You have a town house, I hope? A girl with a simple, unspoiled nature, like Gwendolen, could hardly be expected to reside in the country.

JACK: Well, I own a house in Belgrave Square, but it is let by the year to Lady Bloxham.

LADY BRACKNELL: What number in Belgrave Square?

JACK: 149.

LADY BRACKNELL: (*shaking her head*): The unfashionable side. I thought there was something. However, that could easily be altered.

JACK: Do you mean the fashion, or the side?

LADY BRACKNELL: (*sternly*): Both, if necessary, I presume. What are your politics?

JACK: Well, I am afraid I really have none.

LADY BRACKNELL: Now to minor matters. Are your parents living?

JACK: I have lost both my parents.

LADY BRACKNELL: To lose one parent, Mr Worthing, may be regarded as a misfortune; to lose both looks like carelessness. Who was your father? He was evidently a man of some wealth.

JACK: I am afraid I really don't know. The fact is, Lady Bracknell, I said I had lost my parents. It would be nearer the truth to say that my parents seem to have lost me . . . I don't actually know who I am by birth. I was . . . well, I was found.

LADY BRACKNELL: Found!

JACK: The late Mr Thomas Cardew found me, and gave me the name of Worthing, because he happened to have a first-class ticket for Worthing in his pocket at the time. Worthing is a place in Sussex. It is a seaside resort.

LADY BRACKNELL: Where did the charitable gentleman who had a first-class ticket for this seaside resort find you?

JACK: (*gravely*): In a hand-bag.

LADY BRACKNELL: A hand-bag?

JACK: (*very seriously*): Yes, Lady Bracknell. I was in a hand-bag – a somewhat large, black leather hand-bag, with handles to it – an ordinary hand-bag in fact.

The students can be asked to suggest the questions that Lady Bracknell might put and the suggestions compared with those in the script to see what they reveal about her character. Prediction of this sort can be exploited for language purposes also, with the teacher making use of the occasion to introduce language that is contained in the script. This can be taken a step further on occasion by getting students to role-play or improvise the scripted situation. Again, taking the 'handbag' scene as an example, the students would first of all be told a little about the social standing of Lady Bracknell and her imposing character. At the same time Jack's early background of being found in a hand-bag and his present circumstances (a country house and a town house which is rented out) can be introduced. Students could then be put into pairs and given five minutes to work out a short scene between the two and then asked to show the class what they have prepared. Alternatively, for more able classes, students could improvise the scene in pairs. The students would then be able to compare and contrast their versions with the actual script. Generally speaking, this kind of introduction is of more value than simply explaining the context and theme to the students prior to the reading, and thereby doing the students' work for them. Such interpretation and explanation should be part of the discussion stage later.

4.3.1 Presentation

The presentation of the script can be done in several ways. The least satisfactory way is to simply ask the students to read the play out loud, assigning the various parts at will. This can lead to problems of pronunciation, misinterpretation and embarrassment. Worst of all, the reading may destroy whatever humour or intensity the script contains and render it lifeless as far as the class is concerned. Before reading the play aloud, it is necessary for students to be able to cope with the intonational and other pronunciation features of the script as well as being aware of the interpretative aspects. Even in their mother tongue many people have difficulty adapting to the demands of playreading: with the unfamiliar sounds of a foreign language in addition, the task is far from easy and necessitates adequate preparation.

The best way of presenting a script is by getting students to listen to it. Apart from the fact that scripts are intended for the ear rather than the eye, there is the advantage of associating the written words with a correct pronunciation model from the outset. Tapes of scripted scenes are somewhat rare, but it is perfectly possible for teachers to record their own versions using colleagues or native speakers. Where even this proves impracticable, students can read through the script silently. Should the script be several pages long, the teacher can break it up into smaller units, say two or three pages at a time.

4.3.2 Intepretation

Reference has already been made as to the way in which vocabulary problems can be dealt with (3.1). Here we are concerned with interpretation of the script, of which comprehension forms an essential part. Therefore the teacher should start by checking facts about the situation and characters, eg 'What does Lady Bracknell want to find out about Jack?' 'How did Jack acquire his surname?' Once the teacher is assured that the class has grasped the fundamentals of the situation, the discussion can proceed by means of more subjective questions designed to reveal the inner world of the characters and their feelings, questions such as 'What sort of person do you imagine Lady Bracknell to be?' 'How old might she be?' 'What sort of voice could she have?' In this way students are led to understand not only the surface language but also the aims and feelings behind the language. They will thus be prepared for a dramatic interpretation of the script, even if that interpretation is not always successful. (See Williams [1984] for further discussion of comprehension.)

4.3.3 Pronunciation

As far as language learners are concerned, the rehearsal stage requires considerable input as regards pronunciation. This is an ideal occasion for mastering intonation patterns, for the repetition involved means that the students not only get ample practice but are also likely to assimilate the patterns involved. Pronunciation can be dealt with in different ways, depending on the circumstances and type of script. Where a tape is available, the teacher can use it, pausing after difficult sentences for individual or choral repetition. Otherwise, the teacher can adapt a similar approach by reading out selected lines or sentences for students to repeat, concentrating on those features such as rhythm, stress, phonological or intonational peculiarities likely to cause difficulty.

The benefit of the tape can be seen in the following suggestion, in which the script is divided into smaller sections for pronunciation purposes (eg lines 19 – 29 of the extract from *The Importance of Being Earnest*). After going over the pronunciation in the manner described above, the teacher then asks the students to practise the section in pairs, making sure that they have the chance to take both parts. The teacher then plays through the section on the tape again for the students to compare with their own versions and to underline the overall flow (too much emphasis on individual items can destroy the continuity of the whole) before proceeding to the next section. In this way, also, students are exposed to a correct model at several different moments.

4.3.4 Playreading

The class can now proceed to playreading with the aim of injecting life and meaning into the printed text. A convention needs to be established as to whether to read out the stage directions and if so in what manner. Sometimes stage directions are purely functional and are best omitted, eg 'exit stage left', 'in a whisper'. At other times the stage directions are essential to the structure of the scene and should be read aloud by the teacher or a student, eg 'Mrs Eckersley frowns, stands up, walks to the window and looks out anxiously for her husband'. This brings us to casting, a matter that needs to be handled with discretion, since there will be a conflict between letting everyone have an equal share in the activity and pandering to those more naturally gifted at playreading. In situations where there are a large number of characters it is a good idea to start off with more extrovert members of the class in the main roles and to use their interpretations for comments and subsequent discussion by the group as a whole. Subsequently the roles can be changed around and later readers will have guidelines to follow. Another approach is to divide the class into smaller groups and have each group read through the script simultaneously. This reduces the stress involved in reading aloud in front of the whole class but means that the teacher is less able to monitor and guide the reading.

4.3.5 Acting out

For many classes the playreading stage may be as far as the

teacher wishes to proceed. As we have seen, considerable work could already have been done in terms of vocabulary development, listening or reading comprehension, pronunciation practice and fluency practice in the discussion and reading aloud stages. As was pointed out earlier (1.3), however, there are considerable benefits to be had from acting out the scene or scenes, not only in language terms but also educationally. For example there would be more discussion in order to answer certain questions about the staging of the scene. Would Lady Bracknell be sitting or standing? What about Jack? Would they be formal, sitting/standing upright, or casual in manner, with legs crossed and hands in pockets? Would either of them appear nervous? Would there be any movement during the scene and if so what? The teacher can either pose such questions to the class as a whole or divide the class into groups and let each group decide in their own way.

Reading aloud from a script and attempting to act out a scene are by no means easy and the quicker students can dispense with scripts, the better. Ideally, lessons would be so arranged that the students could memorise the script for homework. However, even in play rehearsals it is seldom as easy as that. In 3.2 and 3.3, suggestions were given as to how to wean students away from the script, in particular the device of reading a sentence then looking up; holding the script by one's side and only referring when necessary; the use of blackboard cues; and making use of a prompter. At this stage the teacher should encourage the students to concentrate more on conveying the intention of the words and less on worrying whether the words are exactly right. Over-anxiety about adhering to the precise words of the script can deaden any sense of drama and make the whole activity ineffective. Directors often make use of improvisation during rehearsals in order to help actors get 'inside' their characters. This technique can be usefully adapted for classes that are sticking to the printed script and not concentrating on the meaning. The teacher can encourage the acting process by insisting on students putting away the script and acting out the scene *in their own words*. Afterwards they can revert to the scripted words and fill in with their own where necessary.

4.3.6 Rehearsals

During rehearsals actors need the comments and criticisms of the director if they are to improve. In the classroom the equivalent of the director's role is usually filled by the teacher. In situations where the class is divided into groups the teacher will have to take the part of a roving director, moving from group to group and giving positive suggestions for improvements. In more experienced classes a director can be appointed for each group and made responsible for the subsequent performance. This has a considerable bonus in terms of developing responsibility and leadership and also in terms of eventual comments about the performance, for the director acts as a filter for any implied criticism of the actors.

4.3.7 Performance

The performance stage should be handled with sensitivity. Indeed, some drama exponents prefer to dispense with performances altogether because of the trauma it can cause participants. However, apart from the educational and language goals mentioned in 2.4, the nature of working on a script means that there will be a sense of incompleteness without a performance of some sort. Indeed, students will often demand one. Teachers should therefore seek to allow students the opportunity of showing their creation to others without forcing reluctant participants to go through a possible ordeal. The teacher can therefore either ask for one or two volunteers to perform to the rest of the class or get groups to perform to each other simultaneously, thereby avoiding the full glare of the whole class.

4.3.8 Evaluation

The performance must be followed by a reaction of some kind. Students will need to be rewarded for the good features and to be guided as to how they might improve. These comments can then serve as a spur to further work on the script with attempts to rectify or improve performances. Let us suppose that the teacher has the class of students practising the 'handbag' scene in pairs and then asks for one or two pairs to volunteer to perform to the rest of the class. He then invites comments from the rest of the class, being careful not to discourage through any negative criticism but trying to highlight successful or desirable features for the class to take note of. One way to deflect criticism of individuals is to allude to the name of the characters: 'Do you think that Lady Bracknell would shout or whisper this line?' 'How would Jack feel when Lady Bracknell reacts about the handbag?', etc. Having laid down guidelines, as it were, the teacher can then ask students to change roles or partners and try the scene again, bearing in mind the points made.

Once students have been taken through a scene in this way, they will gain considerably in their ability to handle a script. Where an extract from a longer play has been used, as in this case, the class can then go on to treat a later scene in the same way, making use of the insights gained into character, and comparing and contrasting the nature of the situations.

4.4 A sample lesson

In contrast to the extract from Oscar Wilde, the script in Example 20 is a short sketch specially written for EFL students. The various complaints and illnesses allow for 'acting' of a limited nature, the language is controlled and the unresolved nature of the ending provides the students with some opportunity for invention.

Example 20 Stage two

There are three chairs in a waiting-room.

Enter first patient holding his/her stomach and groaning.
He sits down with a pained expression.
Enter a second patient with backache.

  2 'Morning.
  1 'Morning.
  2 Have you been waiting long?
  1 Not really, but it feels like hours.
5 2 Yes, I know what you mean.
Enter No. 3 with arm in a sling.
  3 'Morning.
  1 + 2 'Morning.
  3 Have you been waiting long?
10 2 Not really, I've only just arrived.
  3 Let's hope we don't have to wait too long.
Enter No. 4 with a limp.
  4 'Morning.
  1 + 2 + 3 'Morning.
15 4 Have you been waiting long?
  1 Quite long.
  2 About ten minutes. (*At the same time.*)
  3 Not too long.
No. 4 looks around for somewhere to sit and sees there isn't anywhere.
20 *He obviously wants to sit down. No. 1 is holding his/her stomach.*

4 You haven't stomach-ache, have you?
1 Yes. It must have been something I ate.
4 It could be food-poisoning. When I had that, the doctor gave me some really horrible medicine that made me feel worse. I had to take a week off work.
25 1 Really? (*Looks worried.*)
4 Yes. And then a friend told me to stop eating for a day and just drink water.
4 Of course. If I were you, I'd try it. Anything's better than that medicine.
30 1 Mm. Yes, that sounds a good idea. I'll give it a try. Thanks a lot (*Goes, still clutching stomach.*)
No. 4 sits down and after a moment turns to No. 2.
4 What's your problem?
2 I've got this terrible backache.
35 4 But there's nothing doctors can do about backache! They just give you painkillers.
2 That might help!
4 True, but you really ought to try sleeping on a hard mattress. That would soon get rid of it.
40 2 Are you sure?
4 Yes. I used to have really bad backache until I got a hard mattress. I never had any trouble after that.
2 Mm. I've heard that before. Perhaps that is the best thing. Thanks. (*Goes.*)
45 *No. 4 moves along a seat and after a moment turns to No. 3.*
4 Nothing serious, I hope?
3 It's pretty bad, I was bitten by a dog.
4 Really? That happened to me once. They gave me some injections with a needle as long as my arm.
50 3 What? Oh no, I can't stand injections!
4 And what's worse, I found out afterwards that you don't need them. You can use antiseptic ointment instead. Why don't you go to the chemist and get some?
3 Yes, I think I will. Thanks for the idea. (*Goes.*)
55 *No. 4 puts leg up on other seats, takes out newspapers and gets comfortable.*

4 That's better! Not long to wait now...
Stage by Stage J. Dougill and L. Doherty (Hodder and Stoughton)

Aim
To reinforce the language of illnesses and advice; to promote oral fluency
Level Middle intermediate (It is presumed that the class have already done some work on the type of language involved.)
Method
1. Warm-up exercises to obtain the students' attention and focus their minds on the language area:
    (a) Give the students a written cue (eg 'You've got backache,) which they demonstrate by mime to the rest of the class, who guess what it is.
    (b) Divide the class into two groups: group A are ill (they can decide the illness for themselves) and group B are to give advice. The two groups pair off and interact; at each clap of the teacher's hands the students find a different partner. After about six interactions enquire from group A about the best advice they received.
2. Presentation of the script: the students read through the script silently, then work together in pairs to answer the following questions:
    - How do we know the first patient is in pain?
    - How might the second patient walk?
    - What exactly is wrong with the third patient?
    - What is the third patient concerned about?
    - What kind of person do you suppose the fourth patient to be? Why?
3. Discussion of the answers to the questions above and the possible character-types involved
4. Pronunciation work on particular sentences:
    - 'Have you been waiting long?' (intonation)

- 'It must have been something I ate.' (weak form)
- 'I had to 'takeaweekoff work.' (rhythm and linking)
- 'The doctor gave me some really horrible medicine which made me feel worse.' (stress and intonation)

5 Work on sections:
   (a) Section 1: lines 1–15
   The teacher demonstrates with volunteers in front of the class with three chairs in a row. Hold script and read ahead, looking up when talking. The students try the same scene in groups, changing roles. After 5 minutes the students put away their scripts and act out the scene again.
   (b) Section 2: lines 17–28 (2 people)
   Same approach as above
   (c) Section 3: lines 30–41 (2 people)
   Repeat approach

6 Rehearsal:
   (a) Arrange the students in groups of 5 and appoint a director (to direct and act as prompter).
   (b) Give the students 5 minutes to make up an ending to the sketch.
   (c) Tell the directors to cast the sketch and to begin rehearsing the sketch for possible performance.

7 Performance:
   (a) A volunteer group shows their performance to the rest of the class. The teacher asks the other directors to comment on what aspects they liked and what they might have done differently.
   (b) Each director goes to watch a different group perform and then comments on their performance afterwards.

8 Follow-up homework:
   The students write a parallel script for a scene at the dentist's.

Time
About 90 minutes

4.5 Creating a script

Although scripts offer considerable potential for exploitation in the language classroom, curiously little in the way of published material has been produced. The lack of specially prepared material has led to teachers selecting and simplifying scripts for native speakers. However, even this tactic might not prove suitable because of the cultural framework and references, number of characters or problems of setting. On the other hand, not many teachers have the time, inclination and ingenuity to make up their own script. One possible solution is for the group as a whole to work on the creation of a script, an undertaking that is less daunting than it may appear.

The basis of creating a script in this way is the use of improvisation and brainstorming as stimuli for ideas and material with the script being written up afterwards. This can either be done by the students and corrected by the teacher or written by the teacher himself. In this way the students will have an active interest in the script, for they will have invested their own ideas in its creation, and the language will be the product of a genuine need to meet the requirements of a given situation. As a result, this process of group collaboration encourages the sort of creativity, meaningful use of language and participation that educational theorists of all colours insist on.

Before the class begins, the teacher needs to have an outline idea in mind. This could be based on recent language-areas covered by the class, revising and reinforcing the vocabulary or functions concerned. Another source is to use the plot of a film or novel and simplify it to its barest skeleton. For example *Romeo and Juliet* might reduce to the tale of a boy and girl whose families object to their being in love. The class would then flesh out the outline by deciding why the families object and how the children react. The resulting version could well be totally unrecognisable from the original! Here is how work on the idea might proceed.

(a) Introduction

The teacher introduces the idea and the outline and calls for suggestions as to why the families involved might object. These can be solicited from the class as a whole and written on the board or the students can work in small groups and make up a list. Classes used to brainstorming techniques could be given two minutes to see how many ideas they could come up with.

(b) Group work

The teacher sets up small groups to work on a scene and provides them with an outline: the parents of one of the lovers are explaining why they object, when the other lover arrives. The groups will have to decide what happens next. Depending on the capabilities of the class, the groups either act out their idea or a spokesperson tells the class. Minds are concentrated in this type of activity if a deadline is set, say 10 minutes.

(c) Class decision

Under the teacher's guidance, the class choose the version they prefer and there will probably be discussion about possible improvements. This is also an opportunity for the teacher to do some reinforcement or remedial language work on phrases and faults that emerged. The teacher should also start making suggestions for sentences or phrases that will be of use in the writing of the script.

(d) Further group work

The teacher now asks the students to work on the continuation of the play, perhaps a meeting of both sets of parents or a scene with just the two lovers, depending on what was decided for the first scene. This is then worked on in a similar manner and a consensus arrived at as to the course of the play and its ending.

(e) Writing out the script

The overall shape of the script is now agreed.
The teacher elicits the first few lines of the script from the class and puts them up on the board. This helps set the tone and shape of the play as well as providing a stimulus to the students' own version, which can be done in class in pairs or set as homework. In scenarios involving more than one scene the students can be assigned different sections to work on. Eventually, all the versions will need to be seen by the teacher, who corrects the English, makes amendments or additions where necessary, and puts together the final script. Work on the script can then proceed as described in 4.3.

4.6 Putting on performances

The value of drama activities was described in 1.2 and 1.3 where such features as creative collaboration, the development of self-awareness and self-confidence, and the benefits of oral accuracy and fluency were mentioned. Putting on a performance increases the stakes in terms of the educational and language goals concerned. Moreover, the task-element that lies at the base of drama activities finds its ultimate form in the major enterprise of putting on a performance. The discussions, the group work, the rehearsals, the memorisation all have a very real purpose that will stimulate students into a commitment to be successful.

Putting on a performance is a rather different matter to the classroom activities mentioned earlier. As well as such obvious considerations as the costumes and stage, there are also particular performance techniques that the students need to master.

4.6.1 Staging the play

The first matter to resolve will probably be where and how to stage the play. There are basically three types of play area: the *proscenium*, which is the conventional stage at the end of a room with the audience seated in front; the *open stage*, whereby the stage projects into the audience, which is seated on three sides; and the *arena*, where the audience is seated in a circle and the action takes place in the middle. Where teachers have access to a large hall, consideration should be given to which play area best suits the play. More often than not, however, the teacher has little choice.

If a school decides to construct a stage, it would be well advised to make a set of wooden blocks that can be moved into different positions and which provide a large degree of flexibility in terms of staging. A good basis is to have three blocks of $2 \times 1 \times \frac{1}{4}$ m., another five lower blocks of $1 \times 1 \times \frac{1}{4}$ m. and some smaller blocks to add height where required of $1 \times \frac{1}{2}$ m. $\times$ 15 cm.

4.6.2 Preparation

Ways of handling scripts have already been described in 4.3. A similar procedure should be followed in this case, as follows:

> pre-activities to arouse interest
> intensive work on a scene or scenes
> reading through of the script
> discussion and interpretation

By working on the script in this way there is an opportunity for different students to try out different roles. The matter of casting will then be easier with the class able to see who is best suited to which role. Drama groups will often make use of ensemble-building exercises at an early stage to promote a sense of collaboration (2.1). Where groups have come together for the special purpose of putting on a play, such group exercises for group development will be of particular importance. Examples are given in the next chapter (5.2).

4.6.3 Rehearsal

There are two main types of rehearsals used by directors, namely the 'stop-go' and the 'notes' rehearsal. In the early stages the 'stop-go' is used for the main part, whereby the actors run through the scene concerned and the director interrupts whenever he or she notices something wrong or wishes for a change to be made. By repeating the scene over and over again, the faults are slowly ironed out and the action on stage approaches what the director envisages. In the final stages the director will probably make use of the 'notes' rehearsal, in which the actors run through the scene without interruption and the director makes notes, either dealing with the points verbally at the end of the scene or handing slips of paper with various points to the actors concerned.

It may sometimes seem that the play is going to be a disaster because of the lack of acting ability and the seeming impossibility of changing it. There are, however, a few techniques that directors use to improve the quality of the production and these are well worth experimenting with.

(a) Improvising

To reduce stiffness and dependence on the script it is a good idea to tell the students to simply forget about the text and to improvise the scene in their own words.

(b) Trying the scene in different ways

If students are acting artificially or awkwardly, get them to play the scene through in different ways, eg dramatically, underplayed, at different speeds. To make the actors more aware of their positioning and actions, get them to run through the scene without words.

(c) Varying voice levels

To aid audibility or intelligibility ask students to shout their lines in the hope that when they revert to normal their voices will be louder than before.

(d) Exaggerating the stress

Again, if students are not conveying the meaning clearly, tell them to over-emphasise the key words in the sentences.

(e) Question characters in role

In order to combat the lack of emotional depth in the acting, ask actors questions in role, eg How do you feel at this moment? What is it that you really want to say? What would you like to happen? This can be developed by taking the actors in question and setting up role-plays in which the actor behaves as the character would. This helps the actor get inside the character, to understand the inner feelings and thus to portray the character with greater insight (a technique known as method acting).

4.6.4. Performance techniques

During the rehearsal of the play the teacher will need to make the performers aware of various performance techniques.

(a) Blocking

Blocking means that someone is standing in the way of a particular character that the audience should be able to see. Make sure that the students are aware of the danger of blocking, particularly at key moments or for important speeches.

(b) Bunching

Bunching means that actors are too close together instead of filling out the stage. This is a common tendency for amateur actors unused to the space of the stage. The director must insist on distances being maintained, otherwise the scene on stage will look like a private dialogue and not like a public spectacle.

(c) Facing the audience

It is vital for actors to face the audience when in the 'limelight'. The natural inclination of amateurs is to face each other when talking or listening. This not only obscures the face and whatever emotion it is registering but also makes lines less audible. This can be a harder technique to acquire than it might appear, for whereas on stage there is nothing strange about facing the audience and talking to someone behind you, in real life this would not be at all common!

(d) Timing

The most important and the most difficult of performance techniques is timing. Inexperienced actors rush through their lines as quickly as possible, partly because of nerves and partly because of a feeling that the performance is enhanced if the delivery is fast. Make students aware that pauses can be just as important as words. Let them see that characters need time to react to each other and that the audience needs time to take in what has happened.

4.6.5 Costumes and props

The costumes and props that are required will need to be decided upon at an early stage and it helps if one person keeps a list of what is needed. Ideally, the school will have a collection of clothes and objects for drama purposes. The most useful items are small articles of clothing that suggest characters in themselves, eg wigs, hats, scarves, bags, masks, glasses. Apart from the obvious advantage of space, such articles usually fit everyone for size and are not subject to the same restrictions as jackets and trousers. Where such clothes are acquired, it is as well to go for big and baggy rather than tight and pretty for the same reason. While clothes such as dresses are best hung on a dress rail for visibility, the wigs, etc should be put in large cardboard boxes marked to show what they contain. Here is a suggestion for what your acting cupboard should contain.

Dress rail   *Boxes*
Jackets   Wigs   Spectacles
Dresses   Hats   Bags
Blouses   Scarves   Shoes
Coats

Objects
Guns   Bottle of whisky   Magazines
Cigar   Glasses   Bell
Clock   Knives and forks   Whistle
Telephone   Tray   Make-up

Music is a powerful aid to performances. Finding suitable music is another matter, though a record such as Moussorgsky's 'Pictures at an Exhibition' is a valuable asset, for it provides a wide range of music, from frightening pieces such as 'Catacombs' to those evoking a quieter mood like 'Il Vecchio Castello'. Music can be used to set the scene before the action starts or as a background to non-verbal scenes such as setting up stalls for a market.

4.6.6 Appointing a stage crew

Teachers often find it useful to appoint students to be in charge of various aspects of the production. This can help occupy those members of the class who are not in the play or who do not want to take part in the performance. One student can be put in charge of props, for example, while another is the stage manager responsible for the arrangement of furniture before each scene. Another might be prompter, reminding students when they should go on and helping them when they forget lines (although it is hoped that by the time of the production students will be able to ad lib). The role of director will probably be filled by the teacher, although there can be assistant directors also.

Putting on a full-scale production is a major event and a rare one. Most teachers will probably deal with a short script or excerpt in one or two lessons, concentrating on the language involved and discussion of the content. Scripts do offer more than other sorts of texts, however, and it is a waste not to exploit them fully, particularly in the form they are intended for, namely acting out. This may be done in a slapstick manner with the emphasis on fun and play-acting, or it might be handled in a more serious way with the class attempting a serious interpretation. The approach taken will depend on the age and maturity of the students, the teacher and the material.

All in all, with their slices of comprehensible input and their potential for language work, pronunciation practice, interpretation, enactment, improvisation and performance, scripts are a valuable weapon in the teacher's armoury.

Points for consideration:
- the benefits and drawbacks of using scripts
- the main factors in the choice of script
- ways of arousing interest in the script
- presentation of the script
- the value of discussion and interpretation
- how to handle pronunciation work
- the value of playreading
- the educational and language benefits of staging a public performance
- the practicality of creating a script from scratch
- the manner of handling rehearsals
- performance techniques for actors to be made aware of.

5.1 Drama-based lessons without a script

5.1 Working without scripts

Many people associate drama with scripts and, as we have seen in the previous chapter, scripts do lend themselves to language learning purposes. However, both in drama workshops and educational drama participants often make no use of a script whatsoever. The drama workshop developed out of a desire to help actors to improve their skills. Via (1976:17) points out Stanislavski's role in fostering the development of the actor's craft: 'Stanislavski realised that an actor has to learn anew to see and not just to pretend to see, to hear and not just pretend to listen, that he has to talk to his fellow actors and not just to read lines, that he has to think and feel.' To this end, a variety of exercises and activities have been developed to heighten actors' sensitivity and performing ability. In time these activities were marshalled into a cohesive framework, so that during a single session there was a progression from simple warm-up exercises to more complex and demanding activities that required creative and imaginative input from the participants. Later still educationalists saw their value for developing the growth of the individual and made use of them in general education. Thus drama workshop activities have had three main uses:
(a) as a lead-in or aid to work on a script
(b) as an exercise in themselves, as part of an actor's training
(c) as part of general education.

Example 21 A selection of drama workshop activities

1 Physical warm-ups:
   (a) running on the spot
   (b) lying on the floor, relaxing and stiffening parts of the body.
2 Pair and group work:
   (a) staring at one's partner as if there were something wrong with him/her
   (b) throwing an imaginary beach-ball to each other
   (c) making sculptures in pairs, where one person moulds the other into a shape
   (d) mirror exercise (see 2.1) with pairs practising and perfecting a routine to show to others
   (e) mime circle, with one person picking up a box and passing it round the circle for the others to guess what is in it
   (f) one person starting an activity, such as gardening, and the rest of the group joining in with appropriate actions one by one.
3 Improvised sketch: the class is divided into small groups to work on a situation. The groups are given 5 minutes to discuss, 5 minutes to practise and then perform to the rest of the class.

A typical drama workshop will start with ice-breakers and group cohesion exercises and develop into extended role-plays and improvisations, perhaps ending with groups showing each other their creations. There is no set formula and the content can vary considerably depending on the person running the workshop and the nature of the situation. The activities in Example 21 were done with adults at an evening class who had little if any previous experience and who did not know each other very well. The workshop lasted an hour and a half and provided physical and mental stimulation for the participants and a degree of pleasure that comes from working with others on a creative venture. Above all, it helped develop confidence in those who were unfamiliar with work of this kind and who doubted their ability to contribute anything worthwhile. Some drama workshop leaders like to give each session a theme with each exercise exploring a different aspect. This has obvious benefits in providing a sense of coherence, though it runs the risk of restricting both form and content to a narrow field. This point will be taken up in 5.2.

The drama workshop approach has been utilised for educational purposes since the 1950s with advocates such as Peter Slade eager to get away from the traditional concept of school drama as working towards the end-of-term play. For Slade scripts could be harmful because they often led to 'the appalling habit of never getting into the part and of reciting lines whilst grinning at the audience'. (Slade: 1958,90.)

As far as language learning is concerned, the drama workshop approach offers a means of stimulating students into spontaneous speech, providing an opportunity for them to try out the language they have learnt and to explore the parameters of their ability. Of course it is by no means the only way in which practice for oral fluency can be given – conversation and games are alternatives – but drama can provide immense enjoyment and satisfaction due to the involvement it tends to promote.

5.2 Planning the activities

In a well-planned drama-based lesson there will be a general progression from introductory exercises to more extended role-plays and improvisations. The selection of the activities will of course depend on the nature of the class, the age of the students, the size of class and classroom and the previous experience of the students. Such elements as fantasy, puppets and masks will have more appeal to younger students whereas improvisations based on modern city problems are likely to be of interest to adolescents. Activities involving large crowd scenes or necessitating a lot of space will prove impracticable in certain conditions. Such factors will be determined by the individual teacher: here the concern is with general guidelines for creating drama-based lessons out of warm-ups and extended role-plays or improvisations.

5.2.1 Warm-up activities

The purpose of warm-up activities is to prepare the students both psychologically and physically for the creativity to come (see 2.1). There are numerous exercises of this kind and the teacher's task is to choose the appropriate ones to suit the class and the situation. Some schools or institutions have drama or acting classes where students come together who do not know each other very well if at all. In such instances the class should begin with warm-up activities that will break down psychological barriers and establish a working rapport. A good example is Activity 22 in which students not only learn each other's names fairly fast but also warm to each other through the light-heartedness of the task.

Activity 22 Mime and name chain
Purpose
   Introductions and breaking the ice
Method
1. The students sit in a large circle (or several smaller circles for very large groups).
2. Person A says his/her name and something he/she likes

doing, together with an appropriate mime.
3 Person B (the next in the circle) repeats the name, activity and mime of person A and then introduces him/herself. The exercise continues in this way around the circle. For example:

Person A: I'm John and I like drinking beer. (*mimes drinking a pint of beer*)

Person B: He's John and he likes drinking beer (*mimes drinking a pint of beer*). I'm Amanda and I like gardening. (*mimes digging the garden*)

Person C: He's John and he likes drinking beer. (*mimes drinking a pint of beer*) She's Amanda and she likes ... etc.

Duration

Between 5 and 10 minutes, depending on the size of the class

Activity 22 provides an initial introduction to other members of the group that can then be followed up by exercises that allow students to start working together in a relatively undemanding manner. A suitable follow-up to the above might be 'Handshakes' (see 2.1) where students could circulate around the room introducing themselves to each other as if at a cocktail party.

Another approach for language classes unused to drama activities is to start off with activities that concern verbal rather than acting ability. Many drama groups use such kinds of games anyway as a stimulus for creativity and a way of fostering group cohesion. They provide a means of making participants feel comfortable and stimulated before embarking on more demanding work. In this sense they are an easy way into drama activities for those who are nervous or unsure about their capacity to cope. Some teachers may spend up to 50 minutes of an hour-long lesson on activities of this sort, building up confidence and enjoyment and ensuring that the students are not put off by making too great a demand on them before they are ready. Most teachers will be familiar with such games as 'Word Association' whereby students have to say a word related to the one before, eg student A: 'cat'; student B: 'mouse'; student C: 'cheese', etc and the 'Spelling Chain' whereby students have to make a word beginning with the last letter of the previous one, eg student A: 'tree'; student B: 'elephant'; student C: 'teenager', etc. The key factor in games of this type is to ensure that there is a sense of urgency, otherwise the games will drag and will alienate students rather than involve them. The simplest technique to keep things moving at a brisk pace is to allow students a maximum of 10 to 15 seconds before passing on to the next person. Alternatively a clapping rhythm can be established with students having to produce words in the pauses. Activity 23 is a verbal exercise that takes students further down the path of dramatic activities, leading perhaps to work on an improvisation.

Activity 23 Story invention
Purpose
  To promote group cohesion and stimulate creativity
Level
  Lower intermediate upwards
Method
1 The teacher makes up the beginning of a story, for example: 'A young man and his dog were walking through a wood when suddenly...'
2 The teacher then indicates that student A should continue the story in whichever way he/she wants. Student A can add as much as a word, a sentence or two sentences.
3 Student A breaks off and indicates that student B should continue.
4 The story continues until it reaches a natural conclusion or the teacher intervenes and starts a new story. (The class

could then go on to work on an improvisation based on one of the stories – see later in this section.)
Duration
From 10 to 20 minutes

A different sort of way into drama activities is provided by mime, the effectiveness of which was discussed in 2.2. As will be seen later, whole sessions can quite profitably be given over to development of mime: here we are concerned with the potential of simple mime exercises to concentrate students' minds on the matter in hand and to promote group awareness. Because of its silent nature, mime is particularly effective in promoting concentration in groups that tend to be excitable. Furthermore, by dispensing with words during the action the class is able to focus on the quality of the performance, leading later to work on the interpretation of character. Activity 24 shows how the emphasis of the class can be placed on acting and performing skills right from the outset without being at all threatening.

Activity 24 Mime circle
Purpose
  To foster group cohesion; to focus on precise physical movement
Method
1 The students sit in a circle or circles. Student A picks up an imaginary object and passes it to student B, who passes it on to student C, etc all the way around the circle.
2 The students guess what the object was. Comments are invited about the way different students handled the object.
3 Student B picks up an object and passes it around the circle.

The exercise is repeated until everyone in the circle has initiated a mime.

Duration

About 10 minutes

As classes become more familiar with drama activities and with each other, more demanding types of warm-ups can be employed. Sometimes these may well be adaptations of the sorts of exercises mentioned so far: Activity 24, for example, can be developed by asking each person to actually do something with the object before passing it on. However, teachers wanting to work on more intensive collaborative work and to get beyond superficial play-acting might want to turn to the trust and sensitivity exercises mentioned in 2.1. Although they serve a similar function to the warm-ups already mentioned, they have the potential to raise the level of commitment of the group if handled in a proper manner. On the other hand, immature or disruptive students would find ample opportunity to disrupt the serious purpose of such activities. Activity 25 illustrates this point.

Activity 25 Trust game

Purpose

To develop trust among group members

Method

1 The students stand in tightly-knit circles of 5–7 with one student in the middle.
2 Each student in the middle shuts his eyes, turns round several times and slowly falls backwards keeping his legs straight.
3 The person towards whom he is falling has to take his weight and slowly return him to a standing position.
4 The person in the middle then falls in a different direction to be caught once more.

5 After a certain time a different member of the group takes a turn in the middle.

Duration
About 10 minutes

This type of exercise is obviously more suited to groups that are serious about drama activities and that would be aware of its value as far as developing group co-operation is concerned.

To sum up, when selecting warm-ups teachers need to bear the following points in mind:

- the familiarity of the group with each other
- the familiarity of the group with drama activities
- the language demands of the activity
- the type of work to follow (see next section).

5.2.2 Developments

The short warm-ups described above basically serve as preparation for more extended explorations of a theme or situation. These can vary considerably in length and nature and the same criteria as above need to be applied. A typical drama workshop pattern at this stage would be:

activity	Setting up → the activity	group → work	[performance] →	discussion
time (min)	[5]	[20]	[5]	[10]

Though there are any number of possible developments, for the sake of simplicity two basic types are dealt with here:

namely extended role-plays and the creation of scenes or sketches.

Extended role-plays provide the type of activity that language students should easily be able to relate to, given the frequency with which role-plays are employed in textbooks and conventional teaching. A good starting-point is the relatively undemanding and tightly structured 'Objectives role-play' described in 3.4. In this, the students are provided with firm guidelines as to the characters and what they should achieve. A possible next step would be to get the students to work on activities that do not involve such input from the teacher but allow the students more latitude in reaching their own decisions about the characters and their intentions. Activity 26 provides a good basis for the teacher to develop students' awareness of characterisation. The dialogue it is based upon can be adapted to the interests and level of the group but should contain the seeds of conflict.

Activity 26 Open-ended dialogue

Purpose

To give practice in oral fluency; to foster students' awareness of characterisation

Method

1 The students are given copies of an open-ended dialogue of sufficient length and difficulty to present a challenge (example below).
2 The teacher presents a pronunciation model for students to copy.
3 The students read through the dialogue and memorise it. (For ways of memorising see 3.2.)
4 The students are allotted roles and told to decide for themselves what sort of character they are playing and what voice and gesture would be appropriate.

5 The students run through the dialogue without the written text.
6 The students are asked to comment on each other's performances and suggestions are given as to how they might improve
7 The students now run through the dialogue again, this time continuing for as long as possible in role.
8 The teacher compares and discusses what happened in the various groups.

Duration

About 20 minutes

Sample dialogue (intermediate level)

A: Do you have to play that music so loudly?
B: Why shouldn't I? I like it!
A: Well, I don't. Besides, I can hardly hear myself think.
B: Come on, it's not that loud.
C: Look, let him listen if he wants to.
A: And how am I supposed to work?
C: You can work later.

Activities of the sort described in Activity 26 lead into improvisations of a more demanding kind, in that the students themselves make up the content. Initially at least it is a good idea to build up the students' confidence by letting them improvise within the safety of their own groups. Later, groups can be asked to polish their improvisations to show to the rest of the class. Only confident and experienced students can be expected to perform improvisations in front of the class.

The sort of activity that provides a bridge to the group exploration and interpretation of theme that is the goal of drama workshops is provided by Activity 27. The students work in pairs on a creation of a limited nature, providing scope for work on portrayal and performance before the freer and less guided work to come.

Activity 27 Matching lines

Purpose

Fluency practice; to develop confidence and ability to portray improvised scenes

Method

1 Each student is given a line of dialogue to memorise.
2 The students then circulate to find who has the line which matches theirs (see examples below).
3 The teacher checks the students are in the right pairs and then asks them to decide who they are and where they are and to make up a short scene incorporating their lines to show to the rest of the class.
4 The students show their scenes to the rest of the class and comments are sought about the portrayals.
5 The pairs then either work on improving their scenes or are given different lines to work on.

Duration:

About 20–25 minutes

Sample matching lines (intermediate level)

1 There seems to be something wrong with this.
2 That's funny, no one else has complained.
3 You don't want to watch this rubbish, do you?
4 Yes, I rather enjoy it, actually.
5 Your serve again. It hit the net.
6 What do you mean 'it hit the net'?

Groups that have built up a sense of rapport and are able to make use of imagination and creativity will be able to go on to activities that require them to work closely together on short productions. The stimuli for work of this kind can come from any number of diverse sources but they fall broadly into two different types. Firstly, there is the group creation of a sketch based on a limited amount of given data. These data might take the form of lines, objects and/or characters. The task for the students is to combine these seemingly random prompts into a coherent sketch. Activity 28 illustrates how the idea works out in practice.

Activity 28 **Random elements**
Purpose
  Fluency practice; to develop group collaboration and creativity
Method
1 The teacher divides the class into groups of 3 or 4. Each group is allotted at random (eg by choosing a slip of paper) a situation, a place and as many characters as there are group members (see examples below).
2 The groups are set a time-limit, say 15 minutes, to prepare a sketch combining the characters, situation and place.
3 The groups perform to each other.
4 The performances are discussed. Should time allow, the activity is repeated.

Duration
About 30–40 minutes

Sample Elements

Situations	*Places*
A theft	In a restaurant
A quarrel	At a football match
An accident	In a pub
A coincidence	On the beach
An embarrassing event	Watching tennis
A lucky escape	On the tube

Characters
Tom Goodheart, a young teacher
Mrs Jones, a 75-year-old widow
Alice Cooper, a pretty secretary
Mr Plod, the local policeman

Charles Windsurf, a rich playboy
Ted Deadend, an unemployed punk
Mrs Moneybags, a sharp businesswoman

Activities of the kind described above depend upon students interacting with sufficient suggestions and imaginative ideas to create a scene out of virtually nothing. Another approach is for groups to interpret a stimulus in a dramatic form. In this case the stimulus could be anything from paintings and a piece of music to poems, articles or jokes. For language students the added comprehension work involved in working on the latter would be a bonus and the language contained might well serve as a prompt or model for the interpretation. In Activity 29, for example, the language of the written stimulus is used by the students in their performance.

Activity 29 Jokes

Purpose

Fluency practice; to develop group collaboration and intepretation

Method

1 The class is divided into small groups. Each group is given a joke written on a piece of paper.
2 The groups are asked to prepare a sketch based on the joke concerned. A time-limit is set, say 15 minutes.
3 The groups perform to each other.
4 The performances are discussed. Should time allow, the activity is repeated with different material.

Duration

About 30–40 minutes

Sample joke

There are four people flying in a hot-air balloon: an English person, an Irish person, an American and a French person.

(The nationalities can be changed if preferred.) The balloon develops a leak and a discussion is held by those on board, during which it is agreed that someone must jump in order to stop the balloon descending. The American volunteers to jump, saying 'I do this for the glory of America and to protect the free world from Communism' just before jumping. The balloon continues to descend, so the French person steps forward and says 'I do this for the glory of France and for the sake of our wonderful French culture', whereupon he/she jumps out of the balloon. The balloon continues to descend and the English person and the Irish person look meaningfully at each other. Eventually, the English person stands forward and says 'I do this for the glory of England', seizes the Irish person and throws him/her out of the balloon.

Activity 29 can be easily adapted to the capabilities and sensitivities of the class in question by the choice of stimulus. Articles relating incidents have obvious story-lines that can be acted out whereas poems or lyrical passages will present a challenge to more creative and imaginative groups.

So far, the emphasis has been on tailoring the structure and theme of the activity to the level and abilities of the students. When planning drama-based lessons it is also necessary to bear in mind the fundamental principle that conflict lies at the base of drama. Many activities, including some of the ones already mentioned, such as 'Matching Lines', rely upon an element of conflict to be present in the activity in order to stimulate further development. The potential conflict might either lie in the lines or dialogue given to the students to work on or be contained within the situation which is being explored. Where students are required to make up scenes based on a given framework it is important to let them choose the final direction to take. For example, supposing the class were working on the theme of relationships, the teacher might prepare the following situation for students to work on: 'Two parents are introduced to their offspring's new boy-/girlfriend, whom they obviously disapprove of.' Groups will find this sufficient stimulus and the teacher would only deprive the groups of a creative opportunity by adding, for example: 'the new girl-/boyfriend comes from a different background and the parents play on this. The offspring then gets very angry and lectures the parents about their attitudes.' As the students already know the outcome, there would be less excitement and involvement in the task.

5.3 Sample lessons

In this section three sample lessons are presented to show how drama-based lessons can be put together. In each of them participants should have a sense of progression as both language and dramatic demands develop. The samples illustrate types of lessons that might be given to (a) students with little or no previous experience of such work (Beginnings); (b) students with some previous experience or ability to handle drama activities (Clothing); and (c) students who are used to drama activities and to working together (Mime). The assumption is that the students are of mixed ability from lower intermediate upwards and that the class size is between 10 and 20. The language aim throughout is to develop oral fluency.

Lesson 1: Beginnings

Purpose

To introduce students to drama activities

Activities *Minutes*

1 Word association: in a large circle with 15 seconds thought allowed. 8

2 Standing in order: students form three teams: the task is for the teams to see which can stand in order the quickest upon the following prompts: (in order of) age/number of records/number of books read this year/how long it takes to come to school/size of family/cooks the most/drinks the most tea.   7

3 Handshakes (see Activity 1): The students move around the room and greet each other in the manner instructed: 10
   - You're in a good mood.
   - You're surprised to see each other.
   - You've just had some bad news.
   - You're not feeling well.
   - You've just had some good news.

4 Conflicts: 25
   (a) Half the class go outside and are told they are late for an appointment with a friend and to think of a suitable excuse. The other half are told to space out around the room, that they are waiting for a friend who is late and that they are fed up as this is not the first time it has happened. Students pair off and interact. Afterwards pairs briefly describe what happened.
   (b) The activity is repeated, this time with the group outside the room playing the part of a customer wanting to return a defective sweater, and the other group a shop-assistant in a shop that does not take back goods once they have been sold.

Total: 50

Comment

The lesson does not require students to act to any great extent nor does it expose them to performing in front of the whole class. However, it does get them used to the idea of creative language work, of moving around the room and of playing parts.

Lesson 2: Clothing

Purpose

To develop students' capacity for characterisation

Activities

		Minutes
1	Discussion: items of clothing (scarves, shoes, hats, gloves, ties, etc) are spread out on the floor and comments sought as to what sort of people might wear them.	10
2	Handshakes: the items of clothing are given out to the students who wear them and adopt the character the item suggests. The students then circulate and at the teacher's command introduce themselves in character to the nearest person.	10
3	Sketch creation:	
	(a) The students are divided into groups of 5 and items of clothing alloted at random to each group. Groups are then given 15 minutes to prepare a short scene to show to the others, based on characters suggested by the clothes.	20
	(b) The groups perform. Discussion follows as to the relative successes of the performances.	20
	(c) Repetition of activity with the students changing groups.	30

Total: 90

Comment

Clothes are the most powerful stimulus for drama activities, after all 'Kleider machen Leut' (Clothes make people) as the Germans say. The opportunities for trying out characterisation in 'Handshakes' is thus followed up by a variety of sketches based on random elements.

Lesson 3: Mime

Purpose
To develop students' ability to mime

Activities   *Minutes*

1 Guided visualisation: the students shut their eyes and   10
   are told to imagine taking an object out of a box. They
   should be aware of its size, how heavy it is, where
   they are holding it and how it feels. They turn the
   object around in their hands, all the time aware of
   how they are holding the object and how it feels.

2 The mime box (see Activity 6): the students take   10
   something out of a box and pass it to another student
   who must use it in some way.

3 Mirroring (see Activity 4): the students work in pairs   10
   and mirror each other's movements trying to perfect a
   routine that can then be performed to the rest of the
   group. One or two pairs demonstrate what they have
   achieved.

4 Mimed sketch:
   (a) The students work in groups on the preparation of   15
       a mimed sketch based on 'bureaucracy'. They are
       given 15 minutes to prepare and rehearse.
   (b) Then there are performances and subsequent   15
       discussion.

5 Adding words: the groups take another group's mime   30
   performance and develop it by adding words (but are
   mindful of the mimed actions).

                                                         Total 90

Comment
The validity and potency of mime have already been referred
to in 2.2. By working on the development of their miming

ability the students will be unaware of their considerable language practice.

5.4 Handling the activities

Many of the basic guidelines for handling drama activities have already been mentioned in earlier chapters. These include:

- having a well-thought-out plan.
- making sure instructions are clear and understood
- leading by example
- avoiding putting students on the spot
- creating a positive atmosphere
- rearranging class furniture if possible.

In this section the emphasis will be on the role of the teacher during the different stages involved in the drama-based lesson. As we have seen, the drama-based lesson will often involve progressive student participation and creativity. As this process takes place, the role of the teacher will alter somewhat. Whereas the teacher will need to take a central, controlling role during the initial warm-up stage in order to set both the tone and content of the lesson, during the activity the teacher will withdraw from this dominating role and leave the students to develop their own ideas. Later, at the performance stage (if there is one) or during the discussion and evaluation of the activity the teacher will once again take on a leading role. Thus the teacher acts as both initiator and

| teacher-centred | setting up the activities | evaluating the activities |
| student-centred | running the activities | |

concluder with, as we shall see, a considerable number of other roles in between. For the moment we shall consider the basic pattern:

5.4.1 Setting up the activities

The point has been made before in this book but it needs emphasising here: provided the activities have been thought through properly, the most likely cause of their failure is lack of understanding by the students of what they are supposed to do. Clarity of instruction is of such importance that teachers are justified in resorting to the mother tongue, if they are able to do so, in situations where the activity might be difficult to explain and some of the students' comprehension rather weak. Far better, however, would be a practical demonstration. Before embarking on the activities it is also a good idea to check that the students have understood, either by getting them to explain the activity back to you or by having a brief trial run. It helps students if a time-limit is set as this gives an indication of what is required in terms of length or preparation. It can also galvanise participants into fruitful action: the difference in involvement between 'Prepare a sketch incorporating these lines' and 'You have five minutes to prepare a sketch incorporating these lines' can be quite startling. It is also helpful to structure activities by setting time-limits for each part of the process. In cases where students are working on the preparation of sketches, for example, the teacher can set five minutes to discuss ideas, then tell students to start rehearsing for a performance in ten minutes. Such time-limits can always be extended by the teacher (either by letting students carry on over the deadline or by granting them another five minutes), but it is in general better to cut things short than to let them go on too long.

5.4.2 Running the activities

During this stage the teacher will want to encourage student creativity and at the same time monitor the language being used. During this dual role the teacher may have to perform a variety of functions. Heathcote (1984:58) mentions the following:

- the positive withdrawer 'who lets them get on with it'
- the supporter of ideas, as a group member
- the supporter of tentative leadership
- the 'dogsbody' who discovers material and drama aids
- the reflector who is used by students to assess their statements
- the arbiter in argument
- the deliberately obtuse one who requires to be informed
- the encourager who believes that the participants can do it.

Thus it can be seen that teachers who merely instruct and sit back waiting for students to create are neglecting many of their duties. The teacher needs to stimulate and facilitate students' creativity. Where groups are having difficulty getting started, the teacher can initiate a brainstorming session by trying to elicit quick answers to such questions as: Where might the action take place? Who could be involved? What might happen? The intention is to elicit a range of possible answers so that the students can select the most promising. This can be done either at the outset of the activity or at any time during the preparation period if groups appear to be having difficulty. Another feature of this stage is that some groups plump for the first idea to emerge and then declare themselves ready without properly exploring the situation in any depth. In such cases the teacher can stimulate further work by simply confronting the characters concerned with questions such as: Who are you? How old are you? What do you want in the sketch? What are you thinking? How do you feel about what is going on? Such questions about the character's background and inner feelings can start students thinking along lines where a more thoughtful portrayal will emerge.

The other main task of the teacher at this stage is to act as a language informant and monitor. Students may well be searching tentatively for ways of expressing themselves and this is the ideal time for the teacher to provide the required language. It not only meets the need of the student at the moment it arises but will also be repeated at least once in any subsequent performance and possibly several times as the students rehearse. At the same time the teacher will want to step in and correct any glaring errors at an early stage before they are rehearsed, repeated and remembered. However, there is a danger that correction can have an inhibiting effect on the students and that it may interfere with the process of creativity. Teachers therefore need to act with tact in this respect and to refrain from stopping students in mid-flow or seeming to criticise students who need encouragement and praise.

One solution is to use 'hot cards' on which the teacher makes a note of the relevant language point and waits for an opportune moment to slip it to the student in question. This combines a minimum of disruption with personal attention and a written reminder. Other options open to the teacher when monitoring activities are to take mental or written notes to refer to later or to record the whole activity. Of the three the first has the advantage of being the least cumbersome, and the last that of being the most comprehensive. However, mental observations are easily forgotten and teachers can only cope with a limited number. Recording and playing back, on the other hand, can be time-consuming and tedious. The most appropriate method of monitoring, then, is that of pen and paper with a simple note to remind one of the point when referring to it later. The disadvantage is that it may make students uncomfortable if they feel they are being monitored in this way and their every mistake noted. It is likely to inhibit them and so defeat the point of the exercise. For this reason teachers should try to be as unobtrusive as possible when monitoring activities, waiting perhaps for an appropriate moment to make two or three notes rather than writing something down as soon as a student has made a mistake or failed to express himself. Another important point in this regard is for the teacher to note down examples of correct or appropriate language use as well. These can be drawn to the class's attention later, acting as a positive reinforcement for the individual concerned and perhaps leading to further language practice.

5.4.3 Evaluating the activities

At the end of an activity, particularly longer ones, there should be concluding remarks and possibly a discussion. This stage has two main functions: the evaluation of the activity itself and consideration of language involved.

If drama activities are to serve educational as well as language aims, evaluation of the activity is of the highest importance. Handled properly, it helps develop self-awareness, the critical faculty and a desire for self-improvement. These qualities should emerge from the students themselves rather than being imposed by the teacher. In other words, the teacher should be seeking to guide and steer the students towards the point where they are making judgements for themselves rather than simply being told what was good or bad. When comparing two different sketches, the teacher can ask students 'Which did you like better?' 'Why?' and explore the reasons why one was more successful than the other. This has far more value than the teacher telling the class 'The first group were much better because...'

At the same time the teacher should encourage students to assess themselves by asking individuals to comment on their own performances. This is particularly important if the class is to develop further into drama activities. Without such a sense of development classes will soon tire of activities that seem to be done for their own sake only. If, on the other hand, classes sense a greater degree of collaboration, a higher standard of performance and deeper exploration of subject-matter, they are liable to gain satisfaction and the desire to continue further. Self-assessment can be started with non-threatening questions such as: What did you think of the activity: How well did you think you did it? Could you have done it any better, do you think? and develop at a later stage, when students are ready, into more probing questions of the sort: Why did you do it that way? Would a person in that situation really behave like that?.

During the evaluation stage the teacher will be trying to get students to think for themselves. Care should be taken to avoid direct or negative criticism (see the general guidelines in 2.5.14), however, for fear of the inhibiting effect. The upshot of such evaluation should be an improved performance, and the best way of reinforcing what has been said is to repeat the activity straight away to see the benefits and gains. Before looking at ways of overcoming student resistance to the idea of repetition, the language performance during the activity needs to be considered.

As we have already seen, some of the language points will have been dealt with during the creative stage. However, there will be others that the teacher has left until the evaluation stage either because he did not want to disturb the group work or because he felt that the whole class could benefit from the points being made. Moreover, problems may have emerged during performances. Many teachers see this stage as simply an opportunity to point out to students what mistakes they made, eg 'You said "He's working like a doctor," instead of he works as a doctor.' However, there are good grounds for thinking that such corrections have little value in pedagogic terms though there may be a psychological value if students themselves want or expect to hear snap corrections of their language (see Norrish: 1983,117). A more positive approach, and one that is likely to be more effective in language-learning terms, is to produce a correct model and get students to repeat or practise it in the following way:

- 'There was a problem with the way some of the customers spoke to the shopkeeper.' (Teacher refrains from naming any students.)
- 'Now what might the customer say in such a situation?' (Teacher elicits suggestions and writes up a model sentence on the board.)
- 'What might the shopkeeper reply to this?' (Again, suggestions are elicited and a model sentence put on the board.)

Eventually, a complete dialogue is built up, then practised and memorised by the students.

There will be other instances where errors do not lend themselves to such treatment. Sometimes they will be of the type that can be rectified by a simple statement or explanation, for example vocabulary or stress misunderstandings. (The common metathesis 'chicken' for 'kitchen' is one example.) Once such mistakes are pointed out, students may well not make them again. Other mistakes might be of a more fundamental nature and the teacher could well leave these for a later period dedicated to practice of the point in question. Should the teacher overhear several sentences with redundant or omitted articles such as: 'But new road will damage the nature', then the matter clearly needs exploring in greater detail than is warranted in the evaluation stage. (See Norrish: 1983.)

We have already seen that the evaluation stage might be a prelude to further work on the same activity, in which case the language practice and models can be immediately brought into play. There are occasions on which it might prove beneficial for students to repeat the activity in exactly the same format, particularly the shorter warm-up exercises. The 'Handshakes' exercise in Sample Lesson 2 would be a case in point, for students should be able to feel a definite improvement in both their character and language performance if the following pattern has been adopted:

activity { evaluation of character portrayal / consideration of language and language model }   activity repeated

This is not to say that activities should always be repeated: this depends very much on the quality of the first performance. Nor does it mean that activities should simply be repeated in their original form, since students will tire of it and come to resent it in time. A simple tactic is simply to get students to change roles in activities involving role-play. Another is to change the composition of pairs or groups, so that students find themselves working with a different partner or partners. A third change that can be made is to the composition of the activity. For example, in 'Conflicts' in Sample Lesson 1 the activity is repeated but on the second occasion the nature of the conflict is changed by changing the circumstances. As well as these three simple changes, the teacher can also make use of directors from among the students. This works by appointing a director for each group and making them responsible for the group's adoption of whatever dramatic or language points were made in the evaluation.

In situations where the teacher sees potential profit in a number of repetitions of a particular scene (eg where important and newly mastered dialogue is being employed), Activity 30 is both effective and entertaining.

Activity 30 Film director's game
Purpose
To get students to repeat and master useful language; to stimulate an entertaining sketch
Method
1 The students run over the model dialogue in a normal manner.
2 The film director interrupts with words to the effect that the performance was terrible and that it should be done again for the camera but this time much more dramatically.
3 The students perform the scene again but this time overact to an exaggerated degree.
4 The film director again interrupts to say that the whole thing now needs speeding up.
5 The scene is repeated at double-quick speed (as when a film is put on fast-forward).
6 As above, with the director calling for it to be slow/more romantic/as in a Western/happier/sadder, etc as appropriate.
Duration
Anything from 15 to 50 minutes, depending on whether the activity is polished for performance or not

5.5 Simulations

Simulations differ somewhat from the other activities mentioned in this section (see 2.3). Play, which Slade saw as being central to children's drama and imagination and which is an essential ingredient of the creativity of many drama activities, is replaced in simulations by truthfulness to real life. In a simulation of a board-meeting, for example, an agenda and realistic documents would be necessary as well as the correct procedures. In a sketch, merely the suggestion of a board-meeting by means of the seating arrangement and the appellature 'chairman' would suffice. Because of this emphasis on truthfulness to the real world, simulations are more often used with adults than children, whose lack of knowledge and experience would make things problematical.

Not only is there a different emphasis to simulations but they tend to be far lengthier than the activities described so far. The simulations contained in *Eight Simulations* (Jones: 1983) are reckoned by their author to take from one and a half to four hours each. In general, simulations are a major undertaking and require adequate preparation and groundwork. Having said that, however, the similarity in approach between drama-based lessons and simulations, as far as the teacher is concerned, far outweighs the differences. In his book on the subject, Ken Jones (1982) points to four main tasks of the teacher in a simulation. These are

- to ensure adequate briefing
- to supervise the mechanics of the simulation during the event
- to monitor the language of the students
- to co-ordinate the debriefing.

Readers of the previous section will realise how clearly this mirrors the handling of other drama activities. Indeed, monitoring of the language and debriefing were dealt with at some length there. The intention in this section is to concentrate on those aspects that are specific to simulations.

5.5.1 Briefing

If it is the participants' first simulation then there are certain introductory guidelines that should be made clear to them. The first of these is that the students should accept and enter into whatever role they are given, for simulations will not work properly if students are half-hearted or negative about their role. Often simulations provide quite specific details about participants' roles, as shown in Example 22.

Example 22 Details provided for a role in a simulation in *The Bridge* (Eight Simulations by K. Jones)

Burns – contractor

You are the managing director of Collins and Sons, the civil engineering contractors. You believe the design of the bridge is superb and that the price is realistic. You have spent a lot of money doing research and preparing plans, so it is important that the bridge is built to repay this expenditure.

There has been a lot of opposition to the scheme in the press.

Persuade the members of the public to support the plan.

A principal cause of simulations going wrong is that of the student who makes it obvious throughout the simulation that he dislikes the role and dissassociates himself from it.

A successful simulation requires the participants to be involved in a very real way and to suspend disbelief for the duration of the activity. Role-acceptance is crucial. Thus in allocating roles in this particular case, for example, no keen environmentalist should have the role of Burns, whose bridge is environmentally destructive. The danger is that allocation in this way lessens the very concept of role-acceptance through its selectivity, and proponents such as K. Jones therefore advocate random allocation only. Another aspect of maintaining face validity is that the students play the simulation for real. This means that they cannot turn round in the middle and ask the teacher 'What shall we do now?' Such a question should be directed within the convention of the simulation to an appropriate character in the simulation. Moreover, students should not step out of role in any way, even by saying something like, 'No, I didn't mean that.' 'Hang on, let's just go back and do that bit again.' Unlike the other drama activities, simulations do not involve rehearsals.

A second element of the briefing will concern preparation of the participants for the particular simulation in question. This may well take the form of a reading assignment and is usually specified in the controller's notes. It is vital that the teacher has an overall view of what the simulation is about and how it works, otherwise there is the grave possibility that it will run into difficulty. A smooth operation will only ensue if teacher and participants have a clear picture of their situation and task. For this reason it is a good idea for teachers to familiarise themselves with a simulation in advance, either by participating in it with colleagues or by sitting in on a class when it is in use.

The teacher also has to decide to what extent language briefing is necessary. This will obviously depend on the nature of the simulation and the level of the students involved. If there is likely to be a technical area of difficulty, then the teacher should foresee this and give students the necessary practice. To go back to the earlier example of the board-meeting, it could be that students are unfamiliar with the type of normal language associated with agendas and business meetings. Thus language briefing can also help in setting students' minds thinking along the right lines.

5.5.2 Supervision

During the simulation the teacher is in control of the running of the operation, hence the usual designation Controller. The great temptation for the teacher-controller is to interfere in the simulation by giving advice, prompting a participant or correcting a student's language. Providing the briefing was adequate, there should be no need for the teacher to take any part in the discussions involved except to administer documents and take decisions as determined by the controller's notes. The teacher-controller is thus like an umpire, concerned with the rules, regulations and running of the event but adopting a neutral and non-interventionist role as far as the direction and outcome are concerned. This can be somewhat difficult when it is all too apparent that the simulation is not going as smoothly as it might or that students have difficulty in formulating what they want to say. However, it is generally true to say that any intervention by the teacher is likely to disrupt the activity and to distract from the nature of the simulation. Problems that occur with either role or language can be dealt with afterwards.

In order to emphasise the role of the teacher it is best if the students face inwards in their group or groups. In this way the teacher becomes external to the course of the discussion and it is harder for students to look to the teacher for approval or help. At the same time the teacher should try to efface himself as far as possible by hovering or moving silently about the classroom without doing anything that might bring attention to himself. If simulations do go awry, this is usually due to the failure of the participants to accept their role, as mentioned before. The least disruptive manner of dealing with this is to pass the participant concerned a note reminding him of his role and responsibility. This is best done within the nature of the simulation. Thus in the above case of Burns the contractor, the student might get a note from Burns's accountant or a member of the board of directors reminding him of how much the company needs to win the contract. If all else fails, then it is best to call off the simulation, discuss what went wrong and to try again with students in different roles.

5.5.3 Monitoring and debriefing

As was mentioned earlier, the monitoring and debriefing follow the lines mentioned in the preceding section (5.4). Language used during the simulation is monitored by the teacher and points arising are dealt with in the debriefing at the end. The other function of the debriefing is to establish what happened in the various groups (if more than one) and to note successes and failures for future reference. The teacher will also be looking to conclude by relating the activity to real life and emphasising its value in language terms.

Points for consideration:
- the value of working without a script
- a general pattern of procedure of procedure in drama-based lessons
- criteria for selecting warm-up exercises
- ways of developing the lesson
- points to consider when planning and setting up the activities
- the teacher's role during the activities
- the value of discussion after an activity
- the benefit and manner of repeating an activity
- the similarities and differences between simulations and other drama activities
- the teacher's role in the briefing and supervision of the simulation.

Conclusion

With their concern for re-creating real life, simulations (5.5) bring us full circle to the beginning of the book and the principal reason for the use of drama activities, namely the need to bridge the gap between the carefully controlled classroom work and the complexity of language in the outside world. We have seen, too, in the course of the book how drama activities can inject life into what might otherwise be sterile language trapped within the confines of a printed page. Because communication lies at the core of drama activities, they are a natural vehicle for language in use.

Drama activities do more than concern themselves solely with language, however. Their potency in both educational and language terms derives from the fact that they are creative acts articulated through concrete action and as such appeal to the 'whole person' rather than the intellectual or rational aspect. Their application implies that the learner is not only a thinker but an emotional and imaginative person as well. This implication runs like a common thread throughout the activities described. These activities range from simple mime to the creation of a sketch, from role-play in pairs to acting in public. Not only are they involving (have you tried daydreaming in the middle of the miming?) but they should also be enjoyable. If either teacher or student finds an activity threatening in any way, then the lesson is ill-conceived. All of us without exception are capable of some form of role-play, for we all play roles in everyday life. From this common starting-point students can be guided towards an ever-increasing range of drama activities with a corresponding growth in self-confidence and language ability.

There are some who see drama activities as peripheral to language teaching. Those that have read this book will, I hope, take a different view and see them as an essential component of the teacher's skill. A classroom devoid of drama might proceed in a calm and orderly manner but it will lack life. Above all, it may leave students quite unprepared for the challenge of a foreign language situation, full of self-doubt like Guildenstern in Tom Stoppard's play *Rosencrantz and Guildenstern are Dead* when the two central characters are faced with the moment of truth: 'But we don't know what's going on, or what to do with ourselves. We don't know how to *act*.' Guildenstern's teacher evidently made no use of drama activities!

Bibliography

Asher, J J (1982) *Learning Another Language Through Actions* Sky Oaks Productions

Byrne, D (1976) *Teaching Oral English* Longman

Goodfellow, R 'Objectives role-plays' in *Practical English Teaching* February 1982

Hodgson, J and Richards, E (1966, 1974) *Improvisation* Eyre Methuen

Hulton, C 'Cup of coffee, fairy godmother?' in *EFL Gazette* No 76 April 1986 p5

Johnson, L and O'Neill, C (Eds) (1984) *Dorothy Heathcote: collected writings on education and drama* Hutchinson

Jones, K (1982) *Simulations in Language Teaching* Cambridge University Press

Jones, K (1985) *Graded Simulations 2* Basil Blackwell

Krashen, S and Terrell, T (1983) *The Natural Approach* Pergamon/Alemany

Livingstone, C (1983) *Role Play in Language Learning* Longman

Moore, S (1967) *The Stanislavski System* Pocket Books, New York

Morgan, J and Rinvolucri, M (1986) *Vocabulary* Oxford University Press

Moskowitz, G (1978) *Caring and Sharing in the Foreign Language Classroom* Newbury House

Nixon, J (Ed) (1982) *Drama and the whole curriculum* Hutchinson

Norrish, J (1983) *Language learners and their errors* Macmillan

Prodromou, L 'Theatrical and dramatic techniques in EFL' in *World Language English* Vol 4 No 1 1984 pp 76–80

Rixon, S (1986) *Developing listening skills* Macmillan
Rose, C (1985) *Accelerated Learning* Topaz
Savignon, S (1983) *Communicative Competence* Addison-Wesley
Slade, P (1967) *An Introduction to Child Drama* Longman
Stevick, F (1980) *A way and ways* Newbury House
Tomlinson, B 'Language through literature and literature through language' in *EFL Gazette* March 1985 p9
Tomscha, T 'Using Total Physical Response Communicatively' in *Practical English Teaching* Sept 1984
Ur, P (1981) *Discussions that Work* Cambridge University Press
Via, R (1976) *English in Three Acts* University Press of Hawaii
Wallace, M (1982) *Teaching Vocabulary* Heinemann
Watkins, B (1981) *Drama and Education* Batsford
Way, B (1967) *Development through Drama* Longman
Widdowson, H 'Comedy, conflict, conviction – recipe for dialogue success' in *EFL Gazette* May 1985 p7
Williams, E (1984) *Reading in the language classroom* Macmillan

Further reading

This list provides titles of books in addition to those referred to in the text which provide further material and ideas for drama activities.

Banks, R (1985) *Drama and Theatre Arts* Hodder and Stoughton: for the nature and history of drama
BBC English by Radio and Television (1975) *The Play's the Thing* BBC: for scripts specially written for EFL students
Brandes, D and Phillips, H (1979) *Gamester's Handbook* Hutchinson: for practical ideas and material
Case, D and Wilson, K (1979) *Off-stage!* Heinemann: for scripts specially written for EFL students; for sketches incorporating particular language items
Case, D and Wilson, K (1984) *Further off-stage!* Heinemann : as above.
Dixey, J and Rinvolucri, M (1978) *Get Up and Do It!* Longman: for practical ideas and material
Dougill, J and Doherty, L (1986) *Stage by Stage* Hodder and Stoughton: for scripts specially written for EFL students; for sketches incorporating particular language items
Frank, C and Rinvolucri, M (1983) *Grammar in Action* Pergamon: for ways of presenting and practising structures and dialogues
Frank, C Rinvolucri, M and Berer, M (1982) *Challenge to Think* Oxford University Press: as above
Hodgson, J and Banham, M (1975) *Drama in Education* Pitman
Holden, S (1981) *Drama in Language Teaching* Longman
Jones, K (1983) *Eight Simulations* Cambridge University Press
Kerr, J (1977) 'Games and Simulations in English Language Teaching' in *ELT Documents 77* The British Council

Lynch, M (1977) *It's Your Choice* Edward Arnold: for practical ideas and material

Maley, A and Duff, A (1982) *Drama Techniques in Language Learning* (Introduction) Cambridge University Press: for practical ideas and material

McRae, J (1985) *Using Drama in the Classroom* Pergamon: for introducing drama activities into the language classroom; Part One: for ways of treating scripts; Part Two: for authentic scripts for EFL students

Mugglestone, P (1977) 'Role-play' in *ELT Documents 77* The British Council

Peachment, B (1976) *Educational Drama* Macdonald and Evans

Revell, J (1979) *Teaching techniques for communicative English* Macmillan: for ideas for the free stage

Rogers, R (1985) *Six Role Plays* Blackwell

Romijn, E and Seely, C (1979) *Live Action English* Pergamon: for a coursebook based on Total Physical Response

Scher, A and Verrall, C (1975) *100+ Ideas for Drama* Heinemann: for practical ideas and material

Schools Council Drama Project (1977) *Learning through drama* Heinemann

Seely, J (1976) *In Context* Oxford University Press: for introducing drama activities into the classroom

Shackleton, M (Ed) (1985) *Double Act* Edward Arnold: for authentic scripts for EFL students

Smith, S (1974) *The Theatre Arts and the Teaching of Second Languages* Addison-Wesley: for ways of treating scripts and putting on performances

Spolin, V (1966) *Improvisation for the theatre* Pitman: for warm-up activities and improvisations without special reference to language teaching

Stoate, G (1983) *Themes from Life* Harrap: for scripts for playreading and discussion

Stoate, G (1984) *Dramastarters* Harrap: for practical ideas and material

Swan, H A (1983) *Act One/Two/Three* Hulton: for scripts for children

The Bits and Pieces Theatre Group (1984) *Bits and Pieces* Collins: for scripts written specially for EFL students

Watcyn-Jones, P (1978) *Act English* Penguin: for practical ideas and material

Williams, G (1986) *Choosing and Staging a Play* Macmillan: for staging a production

Wright, A, Betteridge, D and Buckby, M (1979) *Games for Language Learning* Cambridge University Press: for ways of presenting and practising structures and dialogues